Ethics for the
Real World

Ethics for the Real World

Creating a Personal Code to Guide Decisions in Work and Life

Ronald A. Howard and Clinton D. Korver

with Bill Birchard

Harvard Business Press
Boston, Massachusetts

Library of Congress Cataloging-in-Publication Data
Howard, Ronald A. (Ronald Arthur), 1934-
    Ethics for the real world : creating a personal code to guide decisions in work and
life / Ronald A. Howard and Clinton D. Korver.
      p.   cm.
   ISBN-13: 978-1-4221-2106-1
   1. Decision making—Moral and ethical aspects. 2. Ethical problems. 3. Moral development. 4. Applied ethics. I. Korver, Clinton D. II. Title.
   BJ1419.H68 2008
   170'.44—dc22

                                                    2007048568

CONTENTS

Skillful Decision Making

Man has a natural aptitude for virtue; but
the perfection of virtue must be acquired by
man by means of some kind of training.

—Saint Thomas Aquinas[1]

THE SEED FOR THIS BOOK was planted in the 1970s. It was sown during a moment of temptation to make the wrong ethical decision. Author Ron Howard, working as a decision-analysis consultant, was asked by a defense contractor to analyze which fighter plane the U.S. Air Force should choose for its fleet. The contract was big, lucrative, and appealing.

The client remarked, "Of course, we all know how the analysis will come out."

Howard raised an eyebrow. Well, no, he had no idea. The contractor's plane might easily be the best choice, but he would have to perform the analysis first. The unmistakable body language from the client, however, suggested Howard should give in to the temptation to skip a thorough analysis. Howard just needed to say yes to manipulating the results, and the contract was his.

Howard realized as never before how technical and financial analyses don't offer all that is needed for smart decisions. He turned down the defense contractor's job; he couldn't be tempted to cheat. But the episode turned him to a provocative question: how does a person systematically analyze situations to make clear and correct ethical decisions?

Years later, after teaching ethics for two and a half decades, he has collaborated with coauthor Clint Korver to put the answer in this book. The gist is this: We must *master ethical distinctions* to enable clear ethical thinking. We must *commit in advance to ethical principles*. And we must *exercise disciplined decision-making skills* to choose wisely.

By learning a new way of thinking, in other words, we can all become skillful ethical decision makers. That is the simple message of this book.

For Starters

We begin our journey when we recognize a common human flaw: for love, money, or other "good" reasons, we often violate our ethics. We lie to, deceive, steal from, or harm others. And the cause is usually the same: faulty thinking. Unless we develop ethical reasoning skills, we get comfortable with transgressions. And we develop bad habits. While we are asleep at the ethical wheel, unhappy surprises almost always follow.

But by breaking bad habits and forming new ones, we can remedy this flaw. We can learn to catch ourselves when starstruck by temptation. Not only can we know and do the right thing; we can transform episodes of temptation to our benefit, and to the benefit of those around us.

The goal of our efforts is straightforward: instead of ceding control to a weakness for ethical compromise, we learn to overcome it.

In the pages ahead, we will first sensitize ourselves to our ethical compromises. Usually such compromises stem from our being only vaguely aware of the scope of our indiscretions. Even an icon of honesty, Abraham Lincoln, compromised the truth more often than popular history allows. In 1858, as he ran for the U.S. presidency, it was often unclear whether he was speaking for or against slavery. Depending on whom he spoke to, and whether he was in the North or South, his messages seemed to contradict each other.

More recently, an icon of military history, Stephen Ambrose, was caught plagiarizing in at least five books. Bestselling author of *Citizen Soldiers* and *The Wild Blue*, he was lionized for his work initially, especially the books on World War II. He was a respected professor and became wealthy from royalties. But by all accounts, he continued to the end of his career to plagiarize. He appeared to sacrifice his character for convenience.

If Ambrose and Lincoln compromised their ethics for personal gain, are any of us immune to this flaw? In fact, most of us are vulnerable, and many times for even less worthy reasons—to dodge embarrassment, to impress friends, or simply to avoid the effort of thinking. In everyday affairs, we often dismiss minor ethical compromises. We slip into thinking that, for all practical purposes, we are ethically above reproach—at least we are *almost* above reproach.

Almost, like the executive who misses an appointment and, embarrassed to admit the truth, tells colleagues he was out sick. Almost, like a manager who inflates a travel voucher to compensate himself for "hardship" on the road. Almost, like a boss who salvages his promotion by assuming credit for a subordinate's work.

Almost ethical but not quite. And we say to ourselves, "What great harm is there?" The harm is not so much in the small ethical mistakes themselves. It is in practicing distorted thought. It is in making a habit of fooling ourselves.

As we begin our journey to more effective and ethical thinking, whether as individuals, leaders, parents, teachers, or others, we may succumb to blurred reasoning. But we will finish with habits that allow us to draw bright ethical lines to consistently guide right action.

A Few Insights

Our experience as teachers and advisors has yielded many insights about ethical decision making. A few are worth mentioning from the start. The first is that people often make ethical choices reflexively. In the throes of a dilemma, when we are short on time or energy to think about tough issues, we let temptation blindside us. And we make snap decisions we regret.

A second insight is that as we rationalize our reflexive responses, we numb ourselves to ethical objections. We make a small compromise that serves as a precedent. That precedent leads to another, and then a third, and so on, until we lose sight of the principles we are violating. We dull our faculty for discrimination. In the worst cases, we put ourselves on a slippery slope to committing serious transgressions.

A third is that our transgressions, contrary to our sense at the time, cause lingering discomfort. On the first day of our ethics classes, we ask students—many of whom have worked for a number of years—to cite an ethically sensitive situation that they have experienced. Many of them come up with a situation for which they feel remorse—a white lie here, a petty theft there. And the most bothersome is when such lapses soured relationships.

The message is that while we often think of ethics as shaping character, it may influence relationships even more. Ethical compromises erect social and emotional barriers between people—barriers that stubborn are hard to discuss. Tainted character is bad enough; strained relationships can be worse. Ethical compromise creates both.

In developing ourselves as skillful ethical decision makers, these three insights will emerge repeatedly. The lesson is that it is better to choose instead of react, to develop sensitivity instead of numbness, and to heed the impact of ethical lapses on relationships.

We Are *They*

Many people we encounter downplay the ramifications of inconsistent ethical conduct, especially when it comes to smaller compromises. On the path to becoming skilled ethical decision makers, however, we will find it helpful to take both big and small indiscretions seriously. Errors in thought are usually the same in both cases.

For example, we may refer to lying as exaggeration, taking creative license, spinning. We may excuse ourselves as being lawyerly, forgetful, or tactful. But when we use euphemisms for such actions, we redefine them as less than wrong. This inculcates a risky thinking pattern, where we cloud our ability to reason—and sometimes erroneously assume the reasoning makes sense to those we deal with.

In a Zogby International poll of eight thousand adults, 97 percent said they consider themselves trustworthy. On the other hand, only 75 percent consider the people they work with and live near trustworthy.[2] Allow us to speculate that the gap between these two figures may reflect more than perception. Behaviors that may seem ethical to us may not be considered so high-minded by people we deal with.

As we stress in the chapters ahead, transgressions crop up in the lives of people across all levels of society. The individuals perpetrating them have all levels of education and work in all professions, trades, and industries. It is counterproductive to think we are not players on a landscape dotted with pitfalls we may stumble into ourselves. Temptation is everywhere—and so is compromise.

One danger is that we will get caught up in a sequence of not just small temptations but big ones. Maybe they will be life changing or life threatening. Faulty thinking can lure us into wrongs we never imagined. Philip Zimbardo, a psychology professor at Stanford University, has for decades studied the genesis of evil. He writes, "Virtually anyone could be recruited to engage in evil deeds that deprive other human beings of their dignity, humanity and life . . . we live with the illusion of moral superiority . . . We take false pride in believing that 'I am not that kind of person.'"[3]

The fact is, we are all that kind of person. *We* are *they*. As we will see in the chapters ahead, through thinking errors, denial, and rationalization, we can all be put in a position of selling our character for a pittance, of sacrificing our relationships for a song. That's yet another reason why it is helpful to take a conscious, systematic approach to breaking risky ethical thinking habits—on even the small things.

Our Prescription

The chapters of this book lay out a plan for that conscious effort. It is a plan to become skilled ethical decision makers.

In the first phase, we develop awareness of ethical temptation and compromise.

- **Chapter 1.** We sensitize ourselves to the most common ethical temptations, to lie, deceive, steal, or harm. Our goal is to become *aware* of these temptations—and the unintended consequences of our transgressions.

In the next phase, we learn how to use ethical logic and principles to foster clear thinking.

- **Chapter 2.** We learn the distinctions necessary to reason ethically: the difference between prudential, legal, and ethical dimensions of an action; between positive and negative ethics; and between the action-based and consequence-based schools of thought. Our goal is to become *thoughtful* about ethical reasoning.

- **Chapter 3.** We learn to identify the ethical principles we have derived, consciously or unconsciously, from our religion, upbringing, and culture. We also learn to identify the gaps where our existing principles give inadequate guidance. Our goal is to become *mindful* of our inner voice.

In the third phase, we learn to make ethical choices.

- **Chapter 4.** We identify the common ethical challenges in our life, evaluate them with ethical reasoning skills from chapter 2, and commit to new ethical principles. Our work is akin to setting up a filing system: once we allocate our ethical challenges to proper folders, we don't have to evaluate them anymore. Our goal is to create an ethical code. We can then use the code to make *disciplined, life-enhancing* decisions.

- **Chapter 5.** We learn the three-step process for creative ethical decision making. We practice clarifying the ethical challenge, generating creative alternatives, and evaluating alternatives to choose defensible, ethical responses. Our goal is to become skilled and *decisive*.

In the final phase, we learn to go beyond ethical basics to using ethics as a lever for better living.

- **Chapter 6.** Instead of using the three-step process just to do the "right thing," we strive to use it to do the "best" thing. We learn to seek the whole truth of our behavior, reframe situations to focus on relationships, and use the "loved one" test. Our goal is to *transform* our personal life through wise ethical choices.

- **Chapter 7.** We learn to do the "best" thing at work as well in our personal lives. We again use the whole truth concept, reframe situations to focus on relationships, and adopt the "loved one" test. Our goal is to *transform* our work life through wise ethical choices.

We all yearn to realize the best in ourselves. What confidence can we have that we are succeeding if we feel uncertain about whether we are making ethical decisions the right way? By developing new thinking habits, we learn how to respond intelligently to ethical challenges and live lives of meaning and integrity.

An Engineering Approach

Many books about ethics focus on weighty and controversial issues that few of us deal with in daily life—abortion, euthanasia, capital punishment, dropping a nuclear bomb. This book, in contrast, focuses on issues that people routinely confront in daily life—white lies, secrets, promises, over-billing, putting others at risk. To this end, this book takes an engineering approach. What is an engineering approach? Engineers start on a project by listing the needs of the people they are serving so that they can deliver a successful product or system. Engineers then use fundamental principles of how people and systems operate to build a practical, satisfying solution.

We have done the same for ethics. We have discovered that people need decision-making tools that (1) offer clear ethical guidance, (2) are broadly applicable to everything from the most common to the most important ethically sensitive situations, and (3) are easy to understand and apply. We then built tools using fundamental principles of ethics and decision making, producing the solution you find in this book.

Engineers like to solve a problem once, not over and over again. That's why the chief component of our solution is a personal ethical code. This code guides action in most ethically sensitive situations. Along with the code, we describe key distinctions and ethical decision-making skills to guide action in circumstances not encompassed by the code. Combined, these principles and tools allow readers to make skillful decisions in a wide variety of ethically sensitive situations.

Put another way, instead of prescribing ethics, the book asks readers to develop their own and to take personal responsibility for them. While our views are periodically evident and ardent, we don't have a corner on right answers. Individuals of every persuasion need to figure out their own ethics according to their own inner voices. This book is a self-help guide, assisting each person in avoiding everyday compromises through better thinking habits.

Because we want readers mainly to engineer their own decision-making capabilities, we urge people to resist the temptation to criticize the ethics of others. While criticism may be tempting, it distracts us from the main job: improving ourselves. The question is not whether the actions we see elsewhere in society are right or wrong. The question is what actions of our own will we embrace or shun. In other words, the goal of the book is for each of us to clarify our own principles. Pointing fingers at others slows our own improvement.

By taking an engineering approach, this book offers a way of learning ethical reasoning that is not available elsewhere. It is an approach growing out of the authors' expertise and experience in decision making. On the one hand, it builds on a foundation of rigorous academic research on the best way to make smart decisions. On the other, it translates complex principles from philosophy and behavioral research to provide a set of practical, lifetime tools for making decisions for personal growth.

A Few Clarifications

Before we get started, it is useful to clarify a few issues that often come up in ethics. The first is the distinction between *moral* and *ethical*. Although many people use the words interchangeably, we do not. For us, *moral* refers to behavior customary in our culture or society—or someone else's culture or society. *Ethical* refers to behavior considered right or wrong according to our own beliefs—no matter the culture or society.

Our parents may tell us that sex before marriage is immoral; our ethics may say it is not, or that it is not an ethical issue at all. Because the usage of the two words is confusing, we minimize the use of *moral*. And by our definition, this book is about ethics, not morals.

A second issue is the question of the scope of our ethical concern. Many people refer to environmental ethics, or the ethics of animal treat-ment, or the ethics of destroying historic sites. While the treatment of the environment, animals, and historic sites is important, we set such issues outside the field of personal ethics. Although harvesting a virgin rain forest may be reprehensible, we do not consider it a question of ethics unless the cutting involves compromises of lying, deceiving, stealing, or harming others. For this book, there must be an "other" involved for a situation to be ethically sensitive.

One crucial question of scope that does arise is how big a circle of concern do we draw around ethical decisions. Do we take into consideration the effects on just our family? Our community? Our company? Our nation? All of mankind? The decisions we make often depend on whose welfare we consider. Who are the stakeholders affected by the decision? How broadly do we want to cast our net? Our decisions about right and wrong must specify which people to include, or which stakeholders fall within the boundaries of our "ethical space."

A third issue is whether the content of our thoughts is an ethical concern. We often hear "Thought is father to the deed." Right thoughts may lead to right action; wrong ones to wrong action. But in our engineered approach to ethics, we concern ourselves only with action. Whether something is ethical or not is all a matter of its effect on others.

Interestingly, we find in our ethics classes that what particularly bothers students is not just memories of transgression. It is also an unease from not being clear about the ethical issues raised by a transgression. Was it really wrong? Why? People are bugged by ambiguity, especially the ambiguity of whether an issue was a matter of ethics to begin with.

In such cases, we offer another distinction, the difference between remorse and regret. When we ethically transgress, we often experience remorse. We may, of course, regret poor decisions that have nothing to do with ethics, but ethical compromises tend to feel different to us emotionally. They sit like a burr in our memory. We try over and over to file them away as experiences consistent with our values and self-image. But they don't seem to fit in the values file; they stand out like stranded objects on the desktop of our mind. It is then, when we feel remorse, that we know we are ripe for learning a new way of ethical thinking.

Our Experience

As authors, we come to the subject of ethics from a unique standpoint. Ron Howard is a professor at Stanford University and director of the Decision and Ethics Center in the Management Science and Engineering

Department. He has taught ethics for twenty-five years. But he is known foremost as an expert in decision making. Over forty years ago, he coined the term *decision analysis* to describe an approach that is now a professional field providing decision assistance in business, medicine, engineering, and personal decisions.

Clint Korver is a serial entrepreneur in Silicon Valley who, as a graduate student in the early 1990s, helped Howard teach ethics classes. He also taught ethics as a visiting professor at Grinnell College. He is an expert in decision making. He is the founder and CEO of DecisionStreet, an Internet company that builds Web-based tools to help people make important life decisions in areas such as health, wealth, housing, and family affairs.

Together, we contribute something unique to the field of ethics. We draw on the wisdom of two separate fields to create one unified process. The combination of the two fields couldn't be more natural, as the challenge of ethics is the challenge to make smart decisions. The contribution by the two of us is in applying the rigorous methodology of our field to ancient ethical concepts. We thereby make the wisdom of the giants of ethical philosophy broadly useful.

Applying decision analysis to ethics offers a new avenue to making ethical decisions. As unskilled ethical decision makers, we can end up shaving off pieces of ourselves in order to live with ethical compromises. But as skillful decision makers, we can embrace our full selves and live simpler, more satisfying lives. Whereas we start our journey to effective ethical thinking with an uncomfortable flaw, we end up correcting that flaw and feeling comfortable in our own skin—and deepening our relationships with friends, family, and coworkers.

CHAPTER 1

Almost Ethical

Waking Up to Compromise

*The chains of habit are too weak to be felt
until they are too strong to be broken.*

—Attributed to Samuel Johnson (English
lexicographer and author, 1709–1784)

L ORI ALTSHULER, Vivien Burt, Lee Cohen, and Adele Viguera probably never expected to see their names on the front page of the *Wall Street Journal*—least of all for an ethical mistake.[1] The four of them are leading physicians at the medical schools of Harvard and UCLA. Altshuler, for example, holds a UCLA-endowed professorship in psychiatry, and she has won several awards for teaching and research. She directs two research programs, for mood disorders and women's health.

But on July 7, 2006, the four physicians earned headline billing on page 1 of the *Wall Street Journal*. They had published research in the *Journal of the American Medical Association*, or *JAMA*, supporting antidepressant use by pregnant women. The ethical lapse: they didn't disclose that they also moonlighted for the makers of the drugs—the likes of Paxil, Prozac, and Zoloft. Altshuler consults with, or receives grants from, at least seven drugmakers, including Eli Lilly, Pfizer, and Bristol-Myers

Squibb.[2] Outsiders could be excused for thinking this lapse was an over-sight of little consequence. But that would not accurately reflect reality. Medical publishing has been roiled for years over lapses in conflicts-of-interest disclosure.[3] *JAMA* expressly forbids nondisclosure, even when authors feel their interests are not in conflict: just seven months before the lapse, editors at *JAMA* explicitly warned authors to err on the side of full disclosure.

In the eyes of some doctors, the transgression was hardly minor, either. Recent research has raised questions as to whether congenital de-fects in newborns increase when their mothers use antidepressants during pregnancy.[4] Some readers of *JAMA* were unhappy because they believed the physicians' work was not bias free.[5]

It would be comforting if we could say the four doctors were rogue physicians. That would validate an age-old truth: bad people infiltrate the ranks of even highly credentialed professionals. But that wasn't so. The authors were tops in their profession. And in a follow-up letter in *JAMA* they expressed regret: "We failed to include disclosures of the financial as-sociations . . . [that] would have provided utmost transparency with re-spect to potential conflicts of interest."[6]

The story of the errant physicians illustrates how even the most ac-complished people can get caught in ethical compromise. Often, they are just not paying attention. It also points to a chilling fact: the same can hap-pen to all of us—if we're not ethically alert and astute.

Ethical compromises both big and small hurt us, and we underesti-mate how much. For one thing, one compromise can lead to another as we let our standards slip. Once we cross one line, we may find it hard to resist crossing the next. We can get started going downhill on the proverbial slippery slope, where each compromise becomes easier, and we fall asleep to their consequences. As we develop bad habits, no matter our accom-plishments and virtues, we may find ourselves in shocking situations.

What causes most people the greatest pain is that compromises cre-ate barriers in relationships. As we engage in ethically questionable acts, we find certain subjects hard to discuss with friends, family, or colleagues. We lose spontaneity and authenticity while socializing. We have to expend energy to maintain our deceits. This effort creates a kind of mental over-head, an ongoing expense, and sometimes an additional investment in more compromises to cover the first one. People sense our distance as we try to cover our tracks, and in turn they distance themselves from us.

Our compromises become all the more of a burden as they erode our sense of integrity. Even if we feel extenuating circumstances justify our acts, we are often embarrassed by them. To protect our pride, we usually try to keep them private—and out of the papers and gossip mill. We may dwell on the errors or block them out. Either way we may find we remember small compromises for years. It's as if they happened yesterday. They weigh on our character.

But we can learn to avoid this lowly road—a road we often choose out of ignorance, carelessness, or just plain convenience. We can choose to spot temptations early and use our newfound awareness as a foundation for skillful ethical decision making. Our journey starts by sensitizing ourselves to the range of compromises we already make, to how deeply caught up in them we are, and to their long trail of consequences for both our character and our relationships.

Temptations to Lie

Most ethical transgressions fall into roughly three categories: deception, stealing, and harming. Although there are many variants, these three encompass most wrongdoing. They also tempt us like the Sirens in Greek mythology: we find it hard to escape all their seductions.

Lying, a form of deception, plays a central role in ethical compromise. We single it out for separate treatment because it appears so commonly in ethical thinking. Lying is defined as telling someone something we know not to be true with the intention of misleading them. It does not include misleading others by mistake, as when we tell a friend we have a car waiting at the airport baggage-claim terminal but later find out our car has been towed.

One indication of the central role of lying in our lives is the number of words we have to describe it. We fib, embroider, doctor, dupe, bend, dress up, cover up, overstate, understate, misinform, misguide, and stretch the truth. We varnish, inflate, embellish, garnish, warp, spin, and gild the lily. If we're serious, we fake, con, perjure, dissemble, distort, and tell baldfaced lies.

Most of us are practiced liars. In one study, 147 college students and community members kept daily diaries of lying. The students reported telling an average of two lies per day, the community members one. None thought their lie telling was serious (although none of them asked the people they lied to).[7]

If we hold a video camera up to our lives, we may be astonished at the incredible sweep of lies on the landscape. If we pan that camera to view the lives of others, we see disingenuousness everywhere. Imagine being in the shoes of the following people, whose stories are based on real events:

- You are a consultant, and you know your bid for phase one of a project, at $300,000, will turn off your client. You could bid $200,000, knowing your client will soon agree to the extra work and expense anyway. You are tempted to understate the cost.

- You are a young engineer, and you can't get a software test to run as specified before an industry trade show. Your manager urges you to run past tapes of the test at the show, pretending that it is a live test. You are tempted to go along.

- You are an entrepreneur seeking money to fund your new start-up. You know venture capitalists chop revenue forecasts by 50 percent. You are tempted to inflate your revenue forecast by a factor of two to compensate for the expected discount.

Whether or not you've ever been in these situations, you no doubt have been in similar ones. Every time, you have probably had at least one very good reason to compromise—and at times you did. You lied. You may feel uneasy about it. You may even be haunted by it.

But you shouldn't feel alone. Using compromise as a helping hand in life has a storied, if seamy, tradition. Even revered leaders lie routinely. They hold their heads high and make the best of it anyway. Why shouldn't the rest of us?

Kenny Rogers, a Detroit Tigers pitcher, threw fourteen scoreless innings in the 2006 baseball play-offs to help his team win a place in the World Series. Fans in game three of the series noticed a brown patch on his left palm, a hint of forbidden pine tar. "It was a big clump of dirt and I wiped it off," he said later, when reporters questioned him.[8] Although

Rogers endured some scathing press, he walked away with a sparkling World Series win.

Serious lying may start in adolescence. In studies of thousands of students by the Center for Academic Integrity, over 70 percent admitted to one or more instances of test cheating, and over 40 percent to some form of plagiarism.[9] But serious lying persists into adulthood. In a study of medical residents, one of three said they would lie to colleagues to avoid swapping shifts. One out of eight said they would fabricate a laboratory value.[10]

If we roll video of our actions from the point of view of others—friends, family, and colleagues—we see a different landscape than when we roll it from our own standpoint. We see better why people's defenses go up—even if our lie is only a "white" one.

Many years ago, an engineering professor was driving to California with his family when he learned a lesson about the shadowy side of lying.[11] At the agricultural inspection station at the Arizona border, an agent asked whether the motor home contained any produce. In fact, he had tomatoes in the refrigerator, but for the sake of expediency, he said, "No." The agent waved him on.

"But Dad," his young son wailed as they pulled away. "We do!"

The son knew that the father knew. The father had lied. For years afterward, as the professor rolled that video in his mind, he regretted that moment with the thought "I've just sold out my principles to avoid a two-minute conversation about tomatoes!" He also sullied himself as a role model—and perhaps laid the groundwork to become the author of this book.

There is a psychological cost to lying. Even if no one else discovers our lies, *we* know. Our lies often clash with the people we would like to be. To reclaim the feeling of alignment between our values and actions, we may trivialize the lies, breaking down the psychic barriers to bigger lies. Lies may seem more necessary, less reprehensible.

Even if we're content living with a soiled self-image, lying can create barriers in relationships because we must be on guard not to betray our lies. One lie, when revealed, casts suspicion on everything else we say. We create an overhead of second-guessing and additional demands by others to show them we deserve their trust. Our friends meanwhile ask, "When else has this happened?"

Especially dangerous are white lies, which we commonly view as trivial, diplomatic, or even well-intentioned untruths. Putting white lies in the category of acceptable ethical behavior condones the same dangerous thinking habits as putting more objectionable untruths in that category. It suggests we should be asking, "What color are my lies?"—as if indulging in lies of lighter shades represents wiser thinking. But the relevant question is, "Are these lies or not?"

Few of us admit to how much a lie benefits us compared to the people we lie to. In a study of lying in romantic relationships, 122 undergraduates documented lies in former romances. Each individual reported on one lie told and another received. The results were consistent: when on the delivering end, people viewed the circumstances of the lie far more favorably than when on the receiving end. They viewed their lies more altruistically motivated, spontaneous, justified by the situation, and provoked by the receiver.[12]

The specific data is revealing: When on the telling end, 32 percent said they lied to avoid upsetting the receiver. When on the receiving end, only 4 percent believed the same thing. When on the telling end, 62 percent said the lie was justified, and when on the receiving end, only 8 percent. On the telling end, 8 percent felt the receiver's anger was justified, and on the receiving end, 57 percent.

If we are the liar, we often understate, in our "cost-benefit analysis," the potential downside. We forget: most people do not like being lied to, regardless of how smart and caring we are. The recipients feel manipulated, put in the dark, cheated out of valuable news about their lives. They feel deprived of control in choosing wisely. They feel taken for stooges.

If we are a recipient and get a lousy haircut and someone is kind enough to tell us, we can have it redone. If we get a cancer diagnosis that is bleak and someone is honest enough to tell us, we can prepare ourselves for coming to terms with our future. If everyone gives us only good news, we don't have the opportunity to weigh alternatives or consider real choices.

Imagine if the dashboard of our car always showed the gas tank was full. While this might help us feel better in the short term—by avoiding the anxiety caused by the gauge showing the gas tank almost on empty—in the long term it denies us the opportunity to learn about and solve small problems before they become big problems. Do we want the dashboards of our relationships—feedback from the people in our lives—to lie?

Although we employ lies, we often don't examine them, and we don't tote up the total of their consequences. We don't see how we put our interests above those of others. We need to wake up to our insensitivity, bad habits, ignorance, and blasé attitudes. Only then can we transform temptations to compromise into chances to build character and deepen relationships.

Temptations to Deceive

Along with lies, there are many other ways to deceive. Deception, in its broader sense, may mean failing to correct an inaccurate impression, feigning ignorance, not telling the whole truth, withholding information, sugarcoating the truth, or overusing tact. Deception is intentionally giving a false impression with or without telling a lie. It includes all forms of misleading in addition to telling lies. Because we sometimes see our deceptions with difficulty, we need to sensitize ourselves to them separately.

Deceptions can be conveyed with words but also through gesture, disguise, inaction, or even silence. We can even deceive with statements that are true, or at least "technically" true. "I did not have sexual relations with that woman, Miss Lewinsky," President Bill Clinton so infamously said.[13]

As humans, we are so practiced at deception that, as with lying, we have a whole vocabulary to express the nuances. We bluff, beguile, gloss over, downplay, puff up, leave in the dark, and hoodwink. We whitewash, sweet-talk, exaggerate, string along, take for a ride, propagandize—and snow.

Here again, if we hold a video camera up to our lives, we may marvel at the landscape of deception. Imagine:

- You are a student who told a good friend last night that you couldn't go to a movie because you had to study. In fact, you just wanted to watch television. At breakfast, your friend asks you, "Did you get a lot of homework done?" And you're inclined to deceptively answer, "Not as much as I'd hoped."

- You are a chief financial officer, and you foresee that plant-closure costs will force your company to report an earnings shortfall.

You're tempted to issue a pro forma income statement that excludes one-time expenses, burying them in the complete financial statements. You even consider issuing a statement: "Earnings for the first quarter were up."

- You are a marketing manager assigned to collect nonpublished prices from all your company's competitors. You are tempted to pose as a prospective customer to make your work easier.

As in the case of lying, every time you've been tempted to engage in such compromises, you probably had good reasons to do so—and sometimes you did. Perhaps you didn't feel great about it, but you didn't lose sleep, either.

As with the company of liars, you're not alone. Consider the story from the opening to this chapter. Not just one, but a group of esteemed psychiatrists didn't deem their affiliations with drugmakers material to readers—despite receiving pay from those makers. Readers and *JAMA* editors disagreed.

Deception, like lying, pervades our society. Public figures seem to rely on deception routinely. By appearing to intentionally mislead others, they encourage the same in those who watch them. Even Honest Abe appeared to use deception. Arguing that Abraham Lincoln was "one of the world's great political propagandists," historian Richard Hofstadter contrasts the text of two of his speeches before the 1860 presidential election.[14] In July 1858, Lincoln spoke in Chicago: "Let us discard all this quibbling about this man and the other man, this race and that race and the other race being inferior, and therefore they must be placed in an inferior position. Let us discard all these things, and unite as one people throughout this land until we shall once more stand up declaring that all men are created equal."

Two months later, in September, Lincoln spoke in Charleston, South Carolina: "I will say, then, that I am not, nor ever have been, in favor of bringing about in any way the social and political equality of the white and black races [applause]: that I am not, nor ever have been, in favor of making voters or jurors of negroes, nor of qualifying them to hold office, nor to intermarry with white people . . . And inasmuch as they cannot so live, while they do remain together there must be the position of superior and inferior, and I as much as any other man am in favor of having the superior position assigned to the white race."

Deception is so widespread in our daily lives that it turns up in surprising places. For example, behavior in science could be expected to be a benchmark of integrity. But in 2005, of 1,768 scientists surveyed, 6 percent admitted to having failed to present data that contradicted their previous research. Over 10 percent withheld details of methodology or results in papers or proposals. Over 15 percent dropped observations or data points from analyses because of a gut feeling the information was inaccurate.[15]

The statistics on deception, like those on lying, almost certainly do not reflect the habits of just bad eggs. They reflect the behavior of people like all of us—behavior among humans who generally respect integrity and honesty. The compromise comes from temptations that arise under pressure from competitors, regulators, managers, and others.

Take the case of Merck's Vioxx pain reliever.[16] In the first large clinical trial of the drug, in 1999, researchers ended the collection of data for heart attacks one month before ending data collection for gastrointestinal bleeding. So in their 2000 paper, they essentially omitted three heart attacks from the data. That lowered the rate of heart attacks from 0.5 percent to 0.4 percent, already much higher than in an older, competing drug (naproxen).

The ramifications? The article, which thus downplayed cardiovascular risks, was Merck's centerpiece for selling the safety of the drug to doctors. The company bought over nine hundred thousand reprints. Only in 2004, when another study showed damning increases in cardiovascular injury, did Merck end Vioxx sales. Although the work of the authors of the 2000 study was amended early on to reflect the higher risks, and the authors were later twice censured by the *New England Journal of Medicine* for excluding the data, Merck kept the drug on the market for more than five years.

As with lying, if we roll the video of our deceptions, the landscape looks decidedly different from the recipient's point of view. Deceptions, like lies, spur others to raise their defenses. The deceptions tarnish our character. They damage relationships.

One form of deception is using words to make things sound better or worse than they are—in other words, using euphemism and (its opposite) cacophemism. George Orwell, in his classic "Politics and the English Language," made the point in his inimitable fashion: "Political language—and with variations this is true of all political parties, from Conservatives to

Anarchists—is designed to make lies sound truthful and murder respectable, and to give an appearance of solidity to pure wind."[17]

Destroying villages and killing the defenseless, Orwell noted, had become "pacification"; imprisonment without trial, "elimination of unreliable elements." Orwell would probably not be surprised that killing innocents today has become "collateral damage"; killing our own, "friendly fire." His comment on politicians who utter tired phraseology still rings true: "The appropriate noises are coming out of his larynx but his brain is not involved." (Nor, of course, is his heart.)

Another special kind of deception can arise from secrets. Some years ago, the professor who lied about tomatoes (the author) was asked by his adult daughter to keep a secret. She told him that the professor's son (her brother), who worked for her husband's company, was about to get laid off. She then asked her father not to reveal this privileged information to his son. He agreed.

At this point his son called to say that now that he had a steady job, he wanted to buy a car. He had found a promising vehicle, and would his father like to join him in seeing and test driving it? This secret put the professor in a bind, but he decided to bite his tongue. He joined his son on the car-shopping expedition; luckily, his son decided not to buy a car before hearing directly about the layoff.

A secret, in the same way as a lie, changes the relationships between tellers and receivers. Secrets transfer information, power, and control to the secret holder. They take it from the person in the dark. Small wonder that those who have been left in the dark feel angry, as the professor's son would have felt if he had made a risky purchase when his father could have stopped him.

Yet another special form of deception is the insincere promise, a promise a person does not intend to fulfill. One of the classic insincere promises is perpetrated during job hunting. We accept a job offer, promise to start on a given date, yet continue to look for other jobs. If we get a better job offer, we are tempted to break our promise on the first, which would show our promise was insincere, and would of course ruin a relationship.

Whether we consider our deceptions good or bad, they are like lies: we often let them go unexamined. We lose track of how much we use them, and we ignore their aftereffects. We need to awake to our level of insensitivity, to continue on our journey to skillful ethical decision making.

Temptations to Steal

A second kind of ethical compromise is stealing. Stealing is appropriating the property of others without permission. This includes outright theft, like shoplifting, embezzlement, or swindling. It also means taking or accepting something that is not ours, or acquiring another's property without permission.

In our everyday lives, stealing most often comprises minor theft: downloading copyrighted digital files, profiting from others' inadvertent mistakes, appropriating incidentals we don't have a real claim to. It also means buying under false pretenses, infringing on other's property, underpaying, overbilling, and borrowing to the point of violating another's trust.

Often we "define down" stealing as mooching, pinching, snitching, filching, encroaching, copping, hustling, scrounging, sneaking, cribbing, and lifting. Hank Greenberg, the former CEO of insurance giant AIG, which overstated assets by $2.7 billion, criticized stricter financial regulation, saying regulators were turning "foot faults" (a tennis reference) into "murder charges."[18]

But when we hold the video camera up from the standpoint of the victim, we once again see a dreary landscape. Imagine:

- You are a consultant on a flight to see a client, to whom you will bill your travel time. You meanwhile spend several hours drafting a plan for another client, and you are tempted to bill the same hours to both clients (double billing).

- You are a student living with three roommates, and you discover a local electronics store will give you a wide-screen television free for ninety days, so long as you return it, saying you don't want it. You are tempted to work as a tag team, each taking a ninety-day turn, together copping a free set for the whole year.

- You are paying a restaurant bill for your family, and the server inadvertently omits a $17 entrée from the tab. You are tempted to ignore the error and consider the mistake a discount (underpaying).

You're probably familiar with these situations. As with the vignettes earlier, every time you've been faced by such enticing opportunities you've probably had good reasons to compromise. If you did, you may still feel uncomfortable about it.

Just as lying and deception transfer power and control (if not value) from victim to perpetrator, so does theft. The thief sees the compromise in a kinder light than does the victim. We can all be seduced more easily when theft remains small, not widely visible, and the victim obscure. That's perhaps why our leaders and role models so often get caught.

If it were fiction, we wouldn't believe it. Representative William Jefferson of Louisiana was caught taking bribes in an FBI sting in spring 2006. The agents actually caught Jefferson on video accepting $100,000. Agents later found $90,000 in cash hidden in frozen-food containers in his freezer. Jefferson maintained his innocence and seven months later was reelected.[19]

If such brazen larcenies slip by, no wonder smaller ones are common. A 2006 Harris Interactive survey showed that more than half of office workers pilfer office supplies—one in twenty even takes home decorations like plants, paintings, and furniture.[20] A National Cable & Telecommunications Association study in 2005 showed one of twenty cable television viewers stole their signal.[21]

Patrick Schiltz, an associate professor at Notre Dame Law School, advises young attorneys destined for large law firms on resisting ethical lapses. He notes that most attorneys will slip into ever-increasing theft. They will start, he says, billing clients for a little extra time, figuring this is a "loan" against future work. They will consider it "borrowing," not "stealing." But as borrowers, they will get steadily sloppier about repaying, and then not repay at all.

"You will pad more and more," Schiltz writes. "You will continue to rationalize your dishonesty to yourself in various ways until one day you stop doing even that. And, before long—it won't take you much more than three or four years—you will be stealing from your clients almost every day, and you won't even notice it."[22]

Temptation to help ourselves to more than our due comes up daily, and few of us have not given in to it. Should we accept that business lunch? Or sports tickets? Or overbill for the hard work on that red-eye flight? We risk making decisions disconnected from our values. The gravest threat, once again, comes not from individual lapses, but from letting our habits go unexamined. Only when we wake from our ethical slumber, can we prepare to transform our ethical behavior.

Temptations to Harm

A third kind of ethical compromise is physical harming. Physical harming is the use of or threat to use violence against another person. It also includes acts that may lead to physical injury of another. As with stealing, most of us don't engage in obvious harming. But we may engage in more common yet subtle behaviors that fall in this category, specifically actions that cause risk of harm to others.

A Colombian student once told the story of an experience in running his father's ranch. He received demands for a huge payment of protection money from ruthless local rebels. He thought the rebels would accept far less, so he sent his foreman with half the amount demanded, as a first step in negotiation. The rebels killed the foreman.

Waking up to harming means recognizing which of our actions put others in harm's way. Through our actions, we may turn a blind eye to harm, incite harm, fail to prevent harm, or deceive others into putting themselves in harm's way. We may also work in companies that make products that harm. Unwittingly, we can aid in all kinds of harm if, as Orwell says, our "brain is not involved."

The question is not always, Have I injured someone? It is more likely, Am I complicit somehow? Did I gamble with someone else's well-being? Did I turn aside, jeopardize, or imperil? Did I see the risk yet blink, wink, dodge, discount, dismiss, or disown? For some of us, the question extends to abortion, suicide, euthanasia, and stem cell research.

Imagine:

- You work for an advertising company. You've just won an account for a new cigarette campaign. You believe tobacco harms people's health; in fact, your uncle died from smoking. You are tempted to stay with the account despite your misgivings about promoting a harmful product.

- You are an ophthalmologist, and you encounter patients whose previous eye surgery was botched by a colleague of yours. Your loyalty to your colleague runs strong, and you are tempted to keep your urge to report him to yourself.

- You have had a few too many drinks at your company's holiday party. It is late, you are expected to be home soon, and few people are on the road. Although your faculties are impaired, you are tempted to drive.

You may not have daily exposure to these situations, but similar ones have probably touched your life. As with the vignettes of lying, deception, and stealing, you probably had good reasons to give into temptation—and you often did.

Ironically, we all instinctively feel that, if we are sensitive to ethical compromise at all, we're certainly sensitive to harm. We may not have the willpower or wakefulness to avoid fibbing to our friends or pinching office supplies at work. But we are always ready to take action—indeed, we are always mindful enough—to rid harm from our lives.

Experience suggests otherwise. Our intellects, our sensibilities, our ethical wills—they numb more easily than we think. Suppose we are a rifle smith who makes high-quality sport rifles. We learn that our rifles have become the favorite of assassins. Do we take stock of the ethical implications of our job?

A simple set of experiments by Stanley Milgram in the 1960s surprised psychologists with how people numb to harm as an ethical issue. Milgram asked twenty-six male volunteers to administer shocks to a random subject to test the value of punishment in improving learning. The volunteers were given control of an electrical-shocking device with a dial calibrated in thirty increments, from 15 to 450 volts. Labels indicated intensity: 195, for example, was "very strong shock"; 450, "danger, severe shock." The volunteers were instructed to shock the learning subject every time he gave a wrong answer (when he failed to match sets of paired words). With each successive round, if the subject gave a wrong answer, the volunteers were instructed to raise the voltage one notch.[23]

What the volunteers didn't know was that the subject was not a volunteer, as they were. He was an accomplice, an actor, who would play along to control the conditions of the experiment. The accomplice didn't react to lower-level shocks, but as the volunteers raised the voltage, the subject showed distress: at 300 volts, pounding on the wall of the room in which he was bound to an electric chair.

Milgram had polled colleagues before the experiment to ask them to forecast results. The experts felt few, if any, volunteers would go beyond "very strong shock." But remarkably, *every* volunteer went at least that far (300 volts), and twelve went all the way to 450 volts, in spite of the subject's apparent agony.

The volunteers were not blind to the subject's pain. As Milgram wrote, they "were observed to sweat, tremble, stutter, bite their lips, groan, and dig their fingernails into their flesh." Under the stress of knowing they were inflicting harm, three volunteers had full-blown, uncontrollable seizures.

The lesson wasn't that the volunteers were sadists—any more than U.S. soldiers at Abu Ghraib prison in Baghdad were sadists. It was that psychologically healthy people will inflict pain on others if they have a very good reason to do so—in this case, simply the sense of responsibility to the experimenter to stick with the experiment.

The volunteers, wrote Milgram, "often expressed deep disapproval of shocking a man in the face of his objections, and others denounced it as stupid and senseless. Yet the majority complied." Ironically, Milgram's experiment would itself be considered unethical today. A "virtual" experiment with volunteers in 2006, however, repeated Milgram's work, with the same results.

Temptations to compromise of this magnitude don't generally come up in everyday life. We encounter small ones or temptations in which we are once- or twice-removed from the victim. Still, we are often given the choice of whether or not to put people in harm's way. Our first step on the road to skillful ethical decision making is to wake up to how we customarily act.

The Tragedy of Desensitization

Milgram's experiment raises a broader question: just how insensitive can we, as ordinary law-abiding humans, become? Milgram conducted his work just after World War II, and the impetus for his experiments stemmed partly from the apparent numbing of many Germans under Adolf Hitler to lying, deception, theft, and harm.

Accounts of Nazi behavior showed that practically no limits existed to ethical desensitization. And this was true not just of soldiers. It was true of highly educated civilian professionals, the leaders of society. Some of the most murderous and bestial work was performed by doctors, engineers, lawyers, and managers—people for whom the brain should be "involved."

The lessons of desensitization revealed were not new, of course. They had been played out many times before—in genocides at the hands of Genghis Khan in Asia and at the behest of the emperor of Japan in China. They were played out after—by Mengistu Haile Mariam in Ethiopia in the 1970s and Slobodan Milošević in Croatia, Bosnia, and Kosovo in the 1990s. But the Nazi experience, so well documented, offers an enduring benchmark.

One dark chapter written by the hands of doctors was the legitimization of state-controlled killing.[24] Decades before the war, a vein of German psychiatric thinking emerged that set the stage for the elimination of "unworthy life"—broadly speaking, people with severe health problems. Psychiatrists argued that the state, not the individual, should control death in these cases. This was for the collective good of the social organism.

Hitler took up this idea, and by 1938, when he received a request by a family for the mercy killing of a severely disabled infant, he was ready to act. He gave authority to his own physician, Karl Brandt, to authorize the killing of the blind, partly limbless child. On behalf of his boss, Brandt absolved attending physicians of responsibility.

This "test case" kicked off the systematic mass murders conducted under two programs, one to kill disabled children, and the other the adult insane. An estimated five thousand children were eventually murdered. In the "T4" program, to kill the adult insane, ninety thousand died. And it was doctors, across Germany, who performed the "euthanasia," by poison gas, by injection, through forced starvation.

How could doctors, of all people, turn their efforts from saving lives to taking them? Because the murders were cast, in a twisted way, as mercy killings, construed as a medical procedure. In fact, according to T4 policy, physicians *had* to run the process. Viktor Brack, head of the "euthanasia" department, even coined a motto: "The syringe belongs in the hand of a physician."

Not all physicians fell for the twisted logic, and not all complied with their patriotic obligation to rid the Reich of "useless eaters." But much of the medical community fell into line. And true to the form of many ethical transgressions, the doctors had (at least) one good reason to turn an ethical blind eye: obedience to authority.

Author and psychiatry professor Robert Jay Lifton interviewed participants much later. One doctor who worked at a killing center remarked,

"The whole system radiated that authority. Like it or not, I was part of it . . . I had no choice. I was in this web—this network of authority."

As doctors went numb to unethical behavior, professionals in other fields did so as well. One of the dark chapters for engineers came as they helped to build the Holocaust's corpse-disposal machine. One of the components was crematoria, comprising furnaces, body-handling equipment, and ventilation systems.

At Auschwitz, an order from the commandant for two four-retort ovens was bid on by several firms, and the winner was I. A. Topf and Sons, an Erfurt heating-equipment firm. Engineers designed ovens to burn fifteen hundred bodies a day. In 1943, Topf technicians even sought a way to make burning more efficient. They experimented with different kinds of coke and corpses, measuring their combustibility.

One of the Topf engineers, Fritz Sander, testified after the war that he had gone so far as to take the initiative in late 1942 to build a better high-capacity crematorium for mass incineration. He had even put in for a patent. In the new design, a conveyor belt carried corpses to the crematorium ovens, where they fell onto a grate and slid into the furnace, where they not only burned but provided fuel for the furnaces.[25]

Sander was asked by a postwar interrogator in 1946, "Although you knew about the mass liquidation of innocent human beings in crematoriums, you devoted yourself to designing and creating higher capacity incineration furnaces for crematoriums—and on your own initiative."

Sander replied, "I was a German engineer and key member of the Topf works, and I saw it as my duty to apply my specialist knowledge in this way to help Germany win the war, just as an aircraft construction engineer builds airplanes in wartime, which are also connected with the destruction of human beings."

Like the physicians in the T4 program, Sander had a good reason to transgress ethically. His colleague, senior engineer Karl Schultze, who designed and installed ventilation systems for the crematoria at Auschwitz, did the same. The refrain of these engineers runs along the same lines.

Schultze said, "I am a German and supported and am supporting the government in Germany and the laws of our government. Whoever opposes our laws is an enemy of the State, because our laws establish him as such. I did not act on personal initiative but as directed by Ludwig Topf. I was afraid of losing my position and of possible arrest."

When circumstances conducive to misbehavior arise, when temptations are put before us, we often don't hold the line as we would like to. We go numb to our own ethical standards. Most people react to Nazi history with the thought "They're not like me." But people in Germany were not much different from those of us in advanced countries today. Germany at the time was scientifically, medically, and artistically a world leader—the land of Beethoven and Goethe. Most of the people running the country were the best and brightest from the best universities.

It would be comforting to say that we are different, that we wouldn't do such things, that we would hold the line. But how do we know? Are we sure we have awakened to the compromises in our own lives?

Time for an Examination

Experience shows that too often we live what Socrates called the "unexamined life." We have within us the makings of reform. We do have an inkling, an inner voice, that speaks to us. Unfortunately, we don't always turn up the volume enough to hear it. We do have an idea of what's right and what's wrong. We just don't listen well enough to see compromises for what they are. The worst of it all is that we doze through opportunities for self-examination and growth.

In some cases, we are simply unfamiliar with the ethical nuances that face us. It's as if we are driving a car for the first time and nobody told us we had to educate ourselves about its workings. We run it for 60,000 miles, and the engine burns out because we didn't replace the oil. When we make this obvious mistake, we wish someone had told us about car maintenance, and we regret our lack of awareness. In ethics, as with cars, we can benefit from reading the owner's manual and increasing our awareness of situations we can address today—before we burn ourselves in the future.

The next chapter is about embarking on the next step, a step to the "examined life." We must go beyond just waking to our insensitivities. We must awaken to *why* we have these insensitivities. A hint to the answer is that we often don't know what we don't know. We are, in other words, unskilled thinkers.

As we continue on our ethical journey, we will see that we may have accepted more falsehoods about ethical behavior than we would like. We need to wake up to the principles of ethical thinking that, up to now, may have escaped us altogether. We need to lift the veil not just on our lies, but on the faulty thinking that leads to them.

➤ Your Turn: A Moment of Remorse

On the first day of our ethics classes, we ask students to recall an ethical decision in their lives that still bothers them. They may not know why, but the episode sits uncomfortably in their memory. It may be small, perhaps a white lie to a friend. Reflect on your own past and come up with a decision that still nags. With this chapter as a guide, identify the category of wrong-doing into which the event falls. Were you awake to the consequences?

CHAPTER 2

Draw Distinctions

Overcoming Faulty Thinking

The evil that is in the world almost always comes of
ignorance, and good intentions may do as much
harm as malevolence if they lack understanding.

—Albert Camus[1]

K URT GERSTEIN WAS A TALENTED ENGINEER in Germany in the 1930s. A devout Christian, he was not easily swept up in the deceptions of the Nazi regime. Just the opposite: although he was a member of the party, he campaigned for keeping the Christian faith alive.[2] So fervent was he that, in 1935, he jumped up in a theater to denounce an anti-Christian scene in a play. In 1936, he distributed eight thousand anti-Nazi pamphlets to state employees.

In December 1940, to the astonishment of family and friends, he took another tack of resistance: he applied to join the Waffen SS, determined to become a whistle-blower among the Nazi elite. He figured that if Nazis could infiltrate church groups to spy on the faithful, he could infiltrate the SS and report truthfully about rumored killings of the adult insane. He wrote later, "I had but one desire: to see, to see clearly into this whole mechanism and then cry it aloud to the whole nation!"

Gerstein got his chance in 1941. By then he was spurred on by outrage over the murder in early 1941 of his own sister-in-law, Bertha Ebeling, in the Nazi euthanasia program. As an SS officer, he then witnessed a trainload of six thousand people arrive in Belzec, Poland, where they were herded into a building and gassed with carbon monoxide. Horrified, he worked to funnel this information to the Allies.

But in time he became a direct agent of harm himself. In 1942, he received orders to buy 100 kilos of prussic acid, the liquid form of cyanide gas. An expert in cyanide disinfection, he knew the order had to be for killing people. Still, he completed this order and at least a dozen more.

Gerstein did impede the killing effort. He destroyed a few shipments of poison gas. He schemed to remove an irritant to make death less painful. In persisting, however, he made what we call a lesser-of-two-evils decision. To combat the evils of Nazi atrocities, he chose to join and publicize the killing effort, hoping to incite the Allies to stop the murder.

In his ethical calculus, Gerstein failed to draw a key distinction—between reasoning and rationalization. His error, highlighted in the extreme, is that he failed to see that the lesser of two evils is still evil. Regardless of his intentions, he became a cog in the death machine. We can speculate that other Germans made the same mistake, all the time thinking, "I do not want to be doing this, yet if I don't, someone else will do it worse."

In daily life, we rarely face ethical decisions loaded with anything like the consequences faced by Gerstein or other Germans. But make no mistake: we routinely face ethical decisions in which we make thinking errors *just like* those of Gerstein. We lie to a friend, urging him to resign from his job, to protect him from a more devious plan by others to oust him. We deceive our spouse or partner about an affair to save them embarrassment.

And if we do not fall for lesser-of-two-evils thinking, we fall prey to other errors that cloud our reasoning. We create "stories" to justify our actions. But our stories serve not to better understand reality but to assuage our consciences. We often realize only after the fact that our stories are awkward. We are unskilled at ethical thinking because we are ignorant of critical distinctions that help us to decide what is right and wrong. That's why, when we make a mistake, we often later wonder, "What was I thinking?"

To Gerstein's credit, he did get word of the gas-extermination program through to the Swedes and the Swiss. He tried to get word to the

Vatican through the church in Germany. But his efforts came largely to naught. The Allies either ignored or disbelieved him.

When the war was over, Gerstein turned himself in to the French. He was confident that when he handed his report to his captors, he would receive a sympathetic hearing, but the French showed little leniency. He died in his cell in Paris, apparently of suicide. We can speculate he realized the evil he perpetrated overshadowed the good.

The Power of Distinctions

Gerstein's story highlights the central role of distinctions in ethical decision making. Distinctions are the keys that unlock understanding. They give us the power to separate the issues of the world into new and useful parts. The better we can discriminate between the parts, the more skillfully we can function as ethical thinkers. Each time we fail to discriminate, we hamper ourselves with a lack of clarity.

Suppose we take our ailing car to a mechanic who opens the hood and says, "There sure are a lot of wires and metal things in there." We would not view these distinctions as very useful in understanding how to fix our car. Or suppose our brain surgeon describes our upcoming operation: "I will be cutting out some of the gray stuff in the front part of your head." Our confidence level sinks. How does the doctor know what to cut and what to leave?

Ethical situations often come with the equivalent of engine wires and gray matter wrapped around the relevant issues. The question we need to answer may be right in front of us, but we can't distinguish it because other parts get in the way—emotional baggage, legal constraints, personal values, work obligations, feelings of loyalty to others, comparisons to peers motivated by envy, and so on.

How do we isolate the question that matters ethically? By arming ourselves with the ability to create new distinctions. We then need to practice making those distinctions, to make them a natural part of our thought process. Some of these distinctions seem obvious when someone else points them out, but they are often hard to see ourselves.

In decision analysis, the most basic distinction we make is simply our choice of words, the building blocks of our thinking. They are the basic units for helping us to discriminate between one thing and another. Learning and using words precisely fosters skillful thought.

During the research for this book, an automated polling company placed a phone call and posed this question: "Do you support the use of unborn babies for stem cell research?" The term *unborn babies* represents a distinction made by the polling company about the definition of a fetus, and that distinction was sure to influence the thinking of people reached by phone. We can guess the polling company chose the word with precision, whereas respondents to the poll may not have been similarly aware of the distinctions embedded in the wording.

Word choice matters. It highlights some elements of a thought and disguises others. If we can agree that words paint pictures, we also have to agree that they put some things in the foreground, some in the back, some in the sunlight, some in the shadows. Often, the trick in making a good decision is finding the right words to paint a situation. The reverse is also true. If we paint carelessly, we make distinctions unwisely.

We can hear echoes of George Orwell's criticisms of the use of loaded words. If we choose value-laden terms, we invoke distortions in thought. If we ask, in effect, "Do you favor killing babies for research?" we start with a distortion. Nobody is in favor of such a thing, so the language draws an unhelpful distinction. If we ask instead, "Do you favor using fetuses in stem cell research?" we get a more reflective answer.

Consciously using the distinctions provided by words is crucial to all varieties of decision making. But there are several other distinctions that are essential in skillful ethical thinking. These include distinctions between:

- Prudential, legal, and ethical dimensions of actions

- Positive versus negative ethics

- Action-based versus consequence-based ethics

- Ethical reasoning versus rationalization

Once we educate ourselves about these distinctions, we will see more clearly the roots of ethical wrongdoing. We will better avoid talking ourselves into doing things we should not be doing. And we take another important step in our journey to becoming skilled ethical decision makers.

Prudential, Legal, or Ethical?

To assess the ethics of any action, it is useful to separate three dimensions of the action: prudential, legal, and ethical. Within the prudential dimension, we distinguish between what is prudent or not prudent; within the legal dimension, between what is lawful or unlawful; and within the ethical dimension, between what is right or wrong. Ethically sensitive situations are often confounded by prudential and legal issues we fail to see. (See figure 2-1.)

An action raises questions in the *ethical* dimension when it pertains to our predefined standards of right behavior. An action in accord with our code of behavior is obviously ethical, and in conflict, unethical. As we saw in the last chapter, the principal issues in the ethical dimension are lying, deceiving, stealing, and harming.

An action raises questions in the *prudential* dimension when it pertains to our self-interest, as in whether we should brush our teeth or refinance our house. An action that is prudential accords with such issues as our notions of financial gain, loyalty to others, friendliness, thriftiness, or just being "nice." We can usually tell we're dealing with the prudential dimension when we balance one issue with another, trade off pluses and minuses, and weigh opposing risks, to decide what the "smart" thing is to do.

FIGURE 2-1

The three dimensions of action

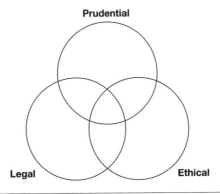

An action raises questions in the *legal* dimension if it pertains to the law in the prevailing social system. Illegal acts obviously include prohibitions such as committing assault, speeding, murder, possessing banned drugs, and spitting in the subway. They do not include acts like being nice to our mother or lying to our neighbor. The law has a coercive aspect: if we break it, society condones physical force, or the threat of force, against us or our property. The law also includes obligations, like paying taxes and serving in the armed forces.

Note how the way we classify an act in one dimension may have no bearing on how we classify it in another dimension. Illegal acts may be prudential. Unethical acts may be prudential. Illegal acts may be ethical. And so on. Conflict is routine, and so is our impulse to let the weight of issues in one diminension override the issues in another. If we are late for an appointment, we may believe that speeding is prudential. If we are hungry and have no money, we may believe that stealing is prudential.

Several years ago church members in the southwestern United States knowingly violated the law. They sheltered illegal immigrants from Central America who they felt were being persecuted in their home countries. Though presumably most members felt this was ethical, we can speculate that for those with families and a lot to lose from arrest and imprisonment, it was not prudential. For those with little to lose—singles without children, say—it was perhaps prudential.

We often fail to distinguish the three dimensions of an action and thus confuse and complicate decisions. One common mistake is to characterize emotionally charged prudential actions as ethically sensitive. Consider the perennial concern of American families of balancing work and life, job and kids. Because many parents consider kids so dear, they construe decisions on spending time with them as ethical. What could be more important than our kids and giving them love and affection?

But as important as these issues are, they are prudential, because we are trading off pluses and minuses, not separating right from wrong. The prudential elements can and do require balancing various practical factors. The error is to impulsively paint these crucial prudential issues as ethical ones because they have the compelling feel of ethical ones. We then think we face an ethical decision—and thus a more complicated decision-making process—when we don't.

The confusion over prudential, legal, and ethical action arises in public life as well. Even before the meltdown of Enron in financial scandal, CFO Andrew Fastow boasted in an interview with *CFO* magazine that he had found numerous inventive ways of reducing Enron's apparent cost of capital. As it turned out, he was often simply shifting debt to off-balance-sheet entities.[3] This was the prudential thing to do for a man who wanted to boost the company's stock price.

But in many cases, Fastow was really engaged in legalized deception. His sleight of hand made Enron's finances look better than they were. Some of his actions, although legal under Financial Accounting Standards Board rules, were clearly unethical. They amounted to lies (misrepresentations) to shareholders and regulators. (Many of Fastow's other moves were simply illegal.)

In one of the classic cases of confusing ethical and legal dimensions, the University of Colorado Buffaloes won a game against the University of Missouri Tigers in 1990 owing solely to an officiating error. As the game clock was running out, officials gave Colorado a mistaken fifth down. Colorado scored a touchdown to win 33–31. Had Colorado not played a fifth down, Missouri would have gained possession of the ball and secured the win by simply running out the clock.[4]

Amid calls to give the win to Missouri, Colorado coach Bill McCartney refused. His action was prudential, retaining the win, and it was legal, at least in keeping with the rule books for college football, because officiating mistakes cannot be reversed after the game ends. But was it ethical? He took something from Missouri that was not Colorado's. As it turned out, the game allowed Colorado to go on and win that year's national college football championship. McCartney let prudential concerns override ethical ones.

The most celebrated case of mistaking legal for ethical action comes from Nazi Germany. In the postwar Nuremberg Trials, one Nazi official after another defended his action as legal and therefore not a crime. The ringleaders of the regime argued again and again that they acted in accord with German law. A senior official and interrogator for the U.S. War Crimes Office put it this way: "They all picture themselves as dutiful little boys who only did what they were told by someone else."[5]

But prosecutors from Allied nations didn't buy this logic. They argued that the laws of a country do not overrule the laws of civilized society, and their reasoning set an enduring precedent. In effect, they said that the legal dimension could not override the ethical. Among the most eloquent was Sir Hartley Shawcross, chief prosecutor for Great Britain and Ireland, who spoke on December 4, 1945. Shawcross, with the Nuremberg judges, rejected the notion that obedience to unjust laws and orders absolved man of responsibility for crimes: "It is no excuse for the common thief to say, 'I stole because I was told to steal,' for the murderer to plead, 'I killed because I was asked to kill.' And these men are in no different position, for . . . it was nations they sought to rob, and whole peoples which they tried to kill . . . Political loyalty, military obedience are excellent things, but they neither require nor do they justify the commission of patently wicked acts. There comes a point where a man must refuse to answer to his leader if he is also to answer to his conscience."

When we become practiced at drawing the distinction between prudential, legal, and ethical dimensions of decisions, we notice something surprising: we encounter ethical dilemmas—situations in which two ethical principles conflict—only rarely. We do not routinely have to decide between two wrongs—for example, between lying and stealing, or cheating and harming. Unlike dramatic scenes in movies, where the action hero has to choose between theft (of a car) and harm (allowing the bad guy to kill his lover), we do not usually get "between an ethical rock and a hard place." Instead, we get between an ethical rock and a prudential hard place.

In other words, we get ourselves into most ethically questionable situations when we are simply tempted to do something wrong. We cheat on a test to get a better grade, bribe a client to make a sale, lie to a friend to save someone's feelings, or misrepresent financial results to prop up a stock price.

When we pick up just about any newspaper, we read about people caught in "ethical dilemmas." But nine times out of ten, they are not dilemmas at all. They are conflicts between prudential gain and ethical action. They are issues of temptation. With practice, we can avoid creating these false dilemmas. We can instead become skilled at peeling away the prudential and legal issues to focus on just the ethical—and making more skillful ethical decisions.

One of the pleasant by-products of this distinction is that we can sometimes reassess the feelings we have about previous actions. Imprudent actions often deserve simple regret. We were stupid, but we weren't "bad." Unethical actions often elicit the more persistent and unpleasant emotion of remorse. When we recognize a past action for the first time as imprudent as opposed to unethical—that is, when we don't get the two confused—we can actually unburden our conscience.

Negative or Positive?

The second useful distinction for skilled ethical reasoning is the difference between negative and positive ethics. Negative ethics are prohibitions that take the form "You shall not . . ." Negative ethics take little or no energy to fulfill. Take "You shall not kill," for example. In everyday life, we don't have much trouble following this principle.

Another characteristic of negative ethics is that they create bright lines. We can easily determine whether we have cheated on a test, killed an innocent person, or lied about having an affair.

Positive ethics are obligations that take the form "You shall . . ." Positive ethics require virtuous behavior, and energy, to fulfill. Take "You shall feed the hungry." Feeding the hungry will require us to go out of our way, and we may struggle with whom to feed, where, and how much. A key characteristic of positive ethics is that they create blurry lines. We often have trouble knowing whether we have fulfilled them.

Because it is hard to draw the lines, we encounter some sticky questions with positive ethics. If we spend $40 for dinner on Friday night, have we acted unethically? Our money could have fed forty hungry people in Africa for a day or more. We risk finding ourselves guilty of unethical behavior. Maybe we should have drawn our lines in a different place. This is the difficulty when our lines leave us discretion.

The danger to clear thinking comes when we treat positive and negative ethics in the same way, out of confusion over their differences. If we treat both with zero tolerance for compromise, we are likely to violate our more ambitious standards for positive ethics. The effect, ironically, is that the challenge of living up to positive ethics actually encourages us to transgress on all our ethical principles.

How can this be? When the going gets tough with feeding the hungry, we are inclined to say something like, "Oh well, discretion is the better part of valor," and back down. Or when we have trouble complying with an ethic to "always return lost property," we say, "Finders keepers, losers weepers," and compromise our principle. Once we no longer consider our positive ethics inviolable, we may start to feel the same way about the negative ones.

More often than not positive ethics are not so much principles as aspirations. They are inherently fuzzy and beg for flexibility in application. If we don't see this, we may encounter an added danger: we will think *all* ethical principles have fuzziness. Ethics begin to feel situational, a balancing of concerns. When this happens, we no longer have any firm ethic to stand on. We become an ethical willow in the wind.

The message is that negative and positive ethics should be thought about differently. We need to be sure to separate in our minds the "shall nots" from the "shalls." This will lead to more judicious articulation of our principles. Instead of thinking we have a positive ethic to feed the hungry, we might think, "I have a positive concern for feeding the hungry." We reclassify an ethic as a concern and can then calibrate our charity to match our energy and resources—without jeopardizing our commitment to skillful ethical thinking.

Actions or Consequences?

The third distinction we must draw for skilled ethical reasoning is perhaps the best known in ethics: the difference between action- and consequence-based decisions. Although moral philosophers take many viewpoints, they divide ethical thinking largely into these two schools. The first was articulated by Immanuel Kant at the end of the Enlightenment in the 1700s and the other by Jeremy Bentham and John Stuart Mill in the late 1700s and 1800s.

Depending on which school of thought we adhere to, we may answer differently to whether an action is ethical or not. The danger of not recognizing the distinction is that we may use both schools of thought, depending on which is convenient, and by alternately using one and then the other, we act as if we have no clear principles at all. If we don't like Kant's answer, we try Bentham's.

Kant felt that ethical responsibility attached to actions, regardless of consequences. Bentham felt responsibility attached to consequences, and actions had to be judged accordingly.[6] In Kant's view, called formalism or deontological ethics, our ethics amount to a set of rigid rules that we wish everyone would follow all the time. Wrote Kant, in 1785, "There is therefore but one categorical imperative, namely this: Act only on that maxim whereby thou canst at the same time will that it should become a universal law."[7]

In action-based ethics, we might choose as our ethical rule to never lie. We would then always tell the truth no matter what we felt the consequences might be. This would seem to fit everyone all the time. In other words, as Kant's formulation requires, the rule would be universalizable.

But problems crop up. Is it ethical to lie to prevent a murder? In Bentham's view, elaborated by John Stuart Mill (the son of a Bentham friend), something is right or wrong depending on the action's consequences. This view stems from Bentham's philosophy of utilitarianism, also called teleological ethics. Bentham believed that an action is ethical if it provides the greatest good for the greatest number.

In the words of Mill, writing in 1861: "Actions are right in proportion as they tend to promote happiness, wrong as they tend to produce the reverse of happiness. By happiness is intended pleasure, and the absence of pain; by unhappiness, pain, and the privation of pleasure."[8]

In consequence-based ethics, we might choose to always tell the truth because honesty generally provides the greatest good for the greatest number. But we would violate the rule when the greatest good dictated that we lie. If we could lie to prevent our brother's murder, we would do so. If we could lie to prevent a terrorist from burning our house of worship, we would do so. If we could lie to make a dying relative happier, we would do so.

As with positive ethics, there are few bright lines with consequence-based ethics. Consider these questions: Would we lie to our spouse to hide an infidelity, to save the family from strife? Would we steal from our employer, to free up the money to pay for children's toys? Would we steal to make good on a donation we pledged to our favorite charity on its 100th anniversary? "It's all for a good cause," we tell ourselves. "The ends justify the means," so long as we don't hurt anyone else.

So the difference between decisions governed by each school of thought can be huge. Given the divergence, how do we decide when our decisions are wrong? It partly depends on the ethics we have adopted beforehand, when we were not in the heat of the ethical battle. Without "preactively" making a decision on right and wrong, we risk impulsively making unethical decisions. We flip-flop from one school to the other. Smart people do it all the time.

Sometimes consequentialism is used to justify laudable goals. Studies show that three-quarters of doctors believe their main responsibility is to act as their patients' advocates, complying with health-care reimbursement rules so long as the rules don't harm their patients. But most doctors, reflecting consequence-based reasoning, still approve of deceiving insurers if payment is initially denied and patients with severe conditions need treatment (bypass surgery, intravenous pain medication). (Note, however, that one-quarter of doctors don't approve of any deception at any time.)[9]

But consequentialism is often used to justify less laudable goals. We don't have to go far to find examples. We overbill a client to make our quarterly billable hours. We lie to our family to save personal embarrassment. We pilfer office supplies to save time. This is a misapplication of Bentham's ideas, however. He meant the greatest good for the greatest number to be a high standard, to encourage people to think about the far-reaching implications of their actions on other people.

To draw the distinction between action- and consequence-based ethics in starker terms, consider a thought experiment. Imagine you are on a plane hijacked by terrorists. One of the terrorists holds the barrel of a gun to the head of the elderly woman beside you and says, "Shoot her." If you don't pull the trigger, killing an innocent passenger, he says he will kill everyone on the airplane.

If you are an action-based thinker, and your principles prohibit killing innocent people, you would not shoot. This may create a tragic situation, but not an ethical dilemma. If you are a consequentialist, the situation becomes much more complex. If you believe shooting your seatmate would save everyone else on the plane, you might conclude that your action (murder) would deliver the greatest good for the greatest number. So you shoot.

But say you are doubtful of the terrorist's intentions, so you don't pull the trigger. The terrorist then shoots the passengers in seats 1A and 1B, and he issues the same command to you again. "Shoot her!" he shouts. What do you do? What is ethical?

Suppose you pull the trigger, thinking, like Gerstein, "I will save all these people." To your surprise, the passengers in seats 1A and 1B get up, take off their bulletproof vests and walk out. Or say that after you shoot, the terrorists still kill everyone on the plane. There are many scenarios. The world is uncertain, and you do not know the future.

But no matter the possibly surprising outcomes, go back to the point when you made the decision to pull the trigger. Was it ethical? Are you now a murderer?

Terrorists may trick us into taking responsibility for their actions, and in so doing cloud our ethical thinking. But the responsibility for our actions always lies with us, because our responsibilities derive from what we can control, and the decisions we can make. Since we do not control the terrorists' actions, their decision to murder is their choice. This is true whether we look at the decision from the point of view of action- or consequence-based ethics. As we like to say, "Only you can make yourself a murderer."

Like many thought experiments, this one is contrived and unlikely, but it shows the differences between the two ethical philosophies. Understanding the distinction is fundamental to making skillful ethical choices. Merely by drawing the distinction correctly, we put ourselves on track to improve decision making. (For a graphical summary of how the distinctions we have learned so far work together, see appendix A.)

Reasoning Versus Rationalization

The fourth distinction we must draw for clear ethical thought is the difference between reasoning and rationalization. Reasoning is a process of analysis for forming judgments. It clarifies the distinction between right and wrong action. Rationalization is a process of constructing a justification for a decision we suspect is really flawed—and often one that was arrived at through a mental process characterized by contrivance and self-dealing. Rationalization purposefully blurs right and wrong.

We can fool ourselves into thinking something is justified when it isn't. This is a lesson we have all learned, probably to our embarrassment. But in ethical decision making, rationalization can become more than an isolated error. It can become a habit. With practice, we can ethically desensitize ourselves to the point that we are likely to repeatedly do the wrong thing. (Think Gerstein.)

When we rationalize, we devise specious but self-satisfying reasons for acting. Or ascribe our actions to high-mindedness when our motives are actually otherwise. Or employ a faulty analogy or wishful thinking. In effect, we create a story that holds together but, upon examination, doesn't hold up.

We commonly rationalize to avoid embarrassment, get ahead, or be kind. When we double-book ourselves and then tell a client we have to break the appointment to see the doctor, we tell ourselves the story that our mistruth preserves an important relationship. When we lie about our software skills in a job interview, we tell ourselves we know we can do the job anyway. When we tell our mother she looks great in a dowdy dress, we tell ourselves our fib will make her feel better about herself.

Euphemism and cacophemism play a central role in rationalization. When we call someone a "terrorist," we may be using a cacophemism—making an activity sound worse than it actually is. When we call the same person a "freedom fighter," we may be using a euphemism—making the activity sound better than it really is. Either way, by using these words we set ourselves up for rationalizing the harming of others.

The telltale sayings of rationalization pop up daily: "If you can't beat 'em, join 'em." "If I don't do it, somebody else will." "It's for the public good." "It comes with the territory." "If it doesn't hurt anyone, what does it matter?" We can be sure that when we catch such lines on the tips of our tongues, we are twisting ethical reasoning.

Prudential thoughts often come in ethical-sounding clothing. Even if we make the right decision, we may have clouded it with spurious thinking. Caught up in prudential concerns, we may buy into the weaker side of ourselves, which is easy to do, because rationalizations abound, they sound legitimate, and we so much want to believe them.

Let's look at one particularly pernicious saying that indicates rationalization: "Everyone else is doing it." We hear it regularly, and we get comfortable with it. In a memo to employees, Warren Buffett, CEO of Berkshire Hathaway and the second-richest man in the United States, singled this phrase out as "the five most dangerous words in business"[10]

There's nothing like the precedent of others, especially when imitated over months or years, to give legitimacy to something. In the IRS Oversight Board survey of taxpayers, four out of ten people say that a belief that neighbors are paying taxes honestly has some or a great deal of influence on whether they report and pay their own taxes honestly.[11] Many taxpayers apparently tell themselves, "If others are massaging the numbers, why shouldn't I do the same?"

The well-known experiments conducted by Solomon Asch half a century ago show how the actions of others can grossly distort our judgment.[12] Asch assembled a group of eight people around a table, all of whom were ostensibly randomly chosen subjects. In fact, all but one were accomplices of the experimenter. On displays, the experimenter posted two pictures. One was of a simple black line. The other was of a set of three lines, one obviously longer, one obviously shorter, and one the same length as the line in the first picture.

The people around the table were then asked to compare the lines. The key question was, in essence, Which of the three lines is the same length as the single line? In response, in one-third of the cases where the seven accomplices purposefully gave the wrong answer, the unwitting subjects agreed. Three-quarters went along at least once. And although some subjects never went along with the group in giving wrong answers, some always went along. Such is the power of "everybody else doing it."

Testing for Rationalization

If we engaged in rationalizations on only the big decisions, we might expect we could catch ourselves simply by being more vigilant. But we rationalize on many small ones as well and so distort our thinking at every level. As a way to distinguish reasoning from rationalization, we can engage in a variety of self-tests. In most cases, one of these tests will force us to remove our prudential-colored glasses:

- **Other-shoe test.** The age-old question: how would we feel if the shoe were on the other foot?

- **Front-page test.** Would we think the same way if it were to be reported on the front page of the *Wall Street Journal?* Or the *New York Times?* Or *USA Today?* Or the paper our hometown friends read?

- **Biased-language test.** Would we feel similarly if we replaced our value-laden language—euphemisms and cacophemisms—with value-neutral language?

- **Role-model test.** Would we do the same if our action exemplified the behavior we would expect from our children?

- **Loved-one test.** Would we change our mind if the person on the receiving end of the ethical transgression were a loved one?

- **Mother's test.** And the simplest of all: what would our mother think?

If we show no interest in asking such questions, we are already on shaky ground. We may be engaging in denial, or we may be letting our emotions get in the way of our thinking. If we feel uncomfortable about a decision—enough that we have to "talk ourselves into it"—we should check to be sure the ethical ground isn't falling away beneath us.

We can guess that Vice President Al Gore, when he was discovered making fund-raising phone calls from the White House in 1997, would have benefited from such questions. He may have used his credit card for the calls, but his action was expressly forbidden, and he certainly knew. In arguing that there was no previous case law to find him at fault, he repeated his famously deceptive (and ridiculed) line: there is "no controlling legal authority."[13]

The Distorting Power of Context

We are especially vulnerable to rationalization and poor ethical thinking when our situation encourages it. Separating our acts from the stage on which we're acting can be difficult. The influence of surroundings—people and place—can push us into doing things that, to observers, appear outright idiotic.

One example of this comes from the Asch experiments. But consider another kind of situation, in which we face the presence of a person in uniform. Unbeknownst to many of us, we learn to make assumptions about uniformed people, and our lifelong indoctrination sticks with us during decision making. Hats, belts, epaulets, insignias, badges, cuffs—these all color our thinking.

Situations often get the better of us, contrary to our considered opinion. No experimenter has shown this better than Philip Zimbardo, the Stanford psychology professor who conducted the classic "prison" experiment in 1971. Zimbardo converted the basement of a Stanford psychology building into a mock prison. He engaged twenty-one psychologically healthy, law-abiding college-age men to participate in the exercise, with the enticement of a $15-per-day paycheck. He randomly divided the men into prisoners and guards, and told all the subjects the experiment would run for two weeks.[14]

The experiment quickly showed how, when we take on the trappings of a particular role, we fall into frightening patterns of behavior. So quickly did the healthy-college-men-turned-guards become abusive that Zimbardo had to end the experiment in just six days. On just the second day, when the prisoners rebelled, the guards drove them from their cell doors with a chilling torrent of fire retardant. The guards then stripped the prisoners naked, removed their beds, and put the ringleaders in solitary confinement.

The abusive treatment escalated even after the prisoners completely submitted to the guards' authority. Zimbardo explained later that the mock uniforms and regimen promoted anonymity, depersonalization, and dehumanization—encouraging abuse just as in a real prison. Zimbardo did not instruct the guards to use forceful, capricious, arbitrary, demeaning, or disorienting tactics. The guards dreamed up such tactics themselves—even though they represented, as Zimbardo said, the "cream-of-the-crop of American youth." In one instance, they made prisoners pick thorns out of blankets dragged through thorn bushes.

Following the experiment, Zimbardo recorded comments by prisoners and guards. The guards recognized they had violated civilized norms. They realized the situation had twisted their thinking. Said one, "I was surprised at myself . . . I made them call each other names and clean the toilets out with their bare hands. I practically considered the prisoners cattle, and I kept thinking: 'I have to watch out for them in case they try something.'"

Overwhelmed by the conditions during the experiment, some prisoners broke into uncontrollable crying, fits of rage, and depression. "The pathology [of guards] observed in this study cannot be reasonably attributed to pre-existing personality differences of the subjects," wrote Zimbardo at the time. "Rather, the subjects' abnormal social and personal reactions are best seen as a product of their transactions with an environment that supported the behavior."

Each subject knew he could, but for the flip of a dime, be in the other man's shoes. Yet the context dramatically influenced his ability to think clearly about ethics. Uniforms, peer pressure, authority, and context all distort our ethical thinking in surprisingly powerful ways. We will find it useful even in everyday living to remain conscious of situational influences.

From Ethical Jungle to Garden

The Zimbardo case makes a powerful point about influences in our environment. But it also makes the larger point of this chapter: if we fail to draw distinctions, we can get trapped in a jungle of ethical errors. Even if we consider ourselves high-minded and virtuous, our minds can take us on a disorienting or terrifying joy ride in the wrong direction. The ultimate danger is that we put ourselves on a slippery slope, and we wake up after having slid much farther downward than we would like.

We can speculate that physicians who murdered the insane in the Nazi T4 program, starting in 1939, failed not just in one moment of drawing distinctions, but in many, over many years, and in many ways. They were often uneasy about their choices, and yet they went along. We can speculate similarly that the engineers who built ovens in the camps at Auschwitz, Dachau, and elsewhere failed in multiple ways over many years.

A T4 physician interviewed by psychiatry professor Robert Jay Lifton after the war noted that no doctor or nurse would have accepted an order to simply kill a child. "I mean if you had directed a nurse to go from bed to bed shooting these children . . . that would not have worked," he said. Instead, the doctors used lethal doses of drugs, and used their powers of rationalization to condone murder. He concluded, "There was no killing strictly speaking . . . People felt this is not murder, it is a putting-to-sleep."[15]

The words of Martin Luther King Jr. are apt: "Nothing in the world is more dangerous than sincere ignorance and conscientious stupidity."[16]

But we don't have to be ignorant about ethical distinctions. We can, step by step, clear a jungle of misunderstanding and replace it with a garden of insight. We can go beyond cultivating distinctions that help us to avoid wrongs, and cultivate distinctions that promote rights. James Allen, the British author of the classic self-help book *As a Man Thinketh* (1918), once described the task at hand: "Just as a gardener cultivates his plot, keeping it free from weeds, and growing the flowers and fruits which he requires, so may a man tend the garden of his mind, weeding out all the wrong, useless, and impure thoughts, and cultivating toward perfection the flowers and fruits of right, useful, and pure thoughts, By pursuing this process, a man sooner or later discovers that he is the master-gardener of his soul, the director of his life."[18]

The skills required to meet the job description of master ethical gardener begin with those in this chapter: Able to distinguish ethical and legal actions from those in our self-interest. Ready to draw a line between negative and positive ethics. Informed enough to commit to action- or consequence-based ethics. Discerning enough to refrain from rationalization. Independent enough to separate our actions from the stage of our acts.

The skills continue with those we will learn in the next chapter, in which we uncover the foundation on which we can base our code of action. We do have a choice on how to act as we become skillful ethical decision makers. And while we will not all agree, we can, and must, find our own benchmarks.

➤ Your Turn: Ethics in the News

Sorting prudential, legal, and ethical issues takes practice. Choose an article from the newspaper that seems to address an ethically sensitive situation. Identify the three dimensions of the decision: prudential, legal, and ethical. Identify any rationalizations used to justify ethically sensitive actions.

CHAPTER 3

Consult the Touchstones

Discovering Our Ethical Principles

At the center of your being you have the answer;
you know who you are and you know what you want.

—Lao Tzu[1]

A LI HASAN, an engineer from the Middle East, had worked for eight years for a U.S. company. Like many young professionals, he was not comfortable with all the practices he encountered in business. What bothered him most: his boss favored nepotism. Hasan felt that this common Middle East cultural practice, whatever its pluses, squelched company excellence. Especially in California's Silicon Valley, friends and family often didn't make the best new hires.[2]

Hasan wasn't thinking just about his own company. He doubted nepotism was ethically right even in his native land. "The Middle East people . . . have a lot of respect for the blood and belief relationships," he said. "Nepotism is very common back home and I hate it." He called nepotism, perhaps with hyperbole, "one of the main factors contributing to the backwardness and destruction of our countries."

In struggling with the question of favoritism, Hasan faced the same challenge we all do: sorting through the collection of ethical principles gathered over a lifetime to decide which ones to call our own. Hasan, a student in our class, whose name we disguise to protect his privacy, realized he had never explicitly questioned which principles he embraced and which he rejected. Just where would he draw the line when he found himself of two minds about right and wrong?

In learning to make clear ethical choices, we all have to examine what we embrace and reject. We must comb through our vast inventory of philosophical, religious, cultural, and social beliefs. Only by holding each up to the light can we decide which ones feel right. Which stem not just from our family's ideals, our religious ideals, our nation's ideals, but from our *own* ideals? Which touchstones will we rely on to create principles in our personal ethical code?

After some study, Hasan reaffirmed his commitment to Islam, whose Shariah prescribes actions as routine as how to walk, talk, eat, and sleep. He also reaffirmed his commitment to virtuous behaviors such as charity. But he couldn't reaffirm all the signals from his cultural breeding. He set aside—as ethically wrong—giving unfair advantage to family and friends in business.

In this chapter, we will explore the mixed chorus of ethical voices emanating from deep within all of us. We will look for the harmonious strains of ethical guidance and separate them from the dissonant ones. This chapter should become a guide to making a list of those principles that inspire us, a list that can then stimulate thinking about other principles that matter.

One caution: we are not searching outside ourselves for prepackaged, off-the-shelf ethics. We are looking for a tailored set of principles that, drawn from the deepest part of our hearts and minds, we have examined and embrace. We will then be able to reaffirm what matters most in our lives, without being thrown off by the crosstalk and static that so often drown out the genuine strains of our inner voice.

When we reaffirm our ethical leanings, we prepare ourselves to commit to principles that allow us to create our ethical code, the subject of the next chapter. By pinpointing the principles we hold dear, consciously or unconsciously drawn from religion, upbringing, and culture, we prepare thoroughly. Only then, when the principles we articulate resonate with our inner voice, can we say we are ready to mindfully follow standards that underpin skillful ethical decision making.

Our Religious Legacy

For many of us, the most prominent strains of ethical guidance come from religion. Whether we have chosen to or not, we have soaked up all manner of principles and rules of thumb from scripture, parables, and stories, derived from prophets, disciples, and sages. Even if we are atheists, we have absorbed teachings woven into our social and cultural fabric.

The first things we absorb in childhood are action-based touchstones. Dictums from religion, for example, generally don't ask us to weigh the consequences before deciding to lie, cheat, or steal. They don't suggest we calculate, in Jeremy Bentham's language of moral philosophy, "the greatest good for the greatest number." They urge an action-based decision, in keeping with Immanuel Kant. As a result, as children, we follow the simple imperative to do what we believe is the "right thing."

The first imperatives we usually consider are negative ones: the "You shall nots." In Christianity and Judaism, negative ethics come from admonitions like those in the Ten Commandments, the most explicit ethical language in the Bible. First in Exodus 20:2–17 and then in Deuteronomy 5:6–21, we read, "You shall not kill . . . You shall not steal. You shall not bear false witness against your neighbor."

In Hinduism, we find similar language. In the first stage of the eight stages of yoga, practices that may date back as much as five thousand years, we find the ten *yamas,* or "restraints." These include *ahimsa* (noninjury), *satya* (truthfulness), and *asteya* (nonstealing).[3]

In Buddhism, we find the "five precepts": "I take upon myself the precept of abstention from killing . . . stealing . . . [and] falsehood."[4]

In Islam, we find similar ethical messages in the Qur'an, fleshed out in the sacred Sunna and later Hadiths. In his Farewell Sermon, in Mecca in 632 CE, the Prophet Muhammad reminded his followers of basic negative ethics. Interestingly, he also warned of the slippery slope: "Beware of Satan . . . He has lost all hope that he will be able to lead you astray in big things, so beware of following him in small things."[5]

Note that not all religious principles are ethical principles. The "shall not" ethical principles are often accompanied by those relating to prudential behavior. In the Ten Commandments we have, "Remember the Sabbath Day." In Buddhism, we have the precept to abstain from "all types of intoxicants causing negligence." In Islam, we have a prohibition of gambling. Though these rules may be important, for most people they are not ethical. We need to be careful not to confuse the two.

We should also be wary of two other sources of confusion. One is that religions, especially Buddhism, emphasize the importance of monitoring our thoughts, not just our actions. But recall from the introduction that "right" and "wrong" thoughts are not ethical issues; only behavior counts. The second is that some religious guidance on ethics is too vague to foster skillful ethical decision making. In the Ten Commandments, we have a refrain common in the world's religions, "Honor your father and mother." But words like *honor* are hard to interpret.

That religious dictums are insufficient for skillful decision making is the lesson of an ancient story from the Hindu *Mahabharata*, the religious world's longest epic poem. In a modern-day formulation of the story, an ascetic (holy man) named Kausika is in the forest when he hears a commotion.[6] He looks up to see a man being chased by a gang of thieves. The man rushes toward Kausika and hides in the bushes behind him. The thieves stop and ask Kausika if he has seen the man. What does Kausika do?

He tells the truth, as his religion would instruct him. The thieves drag the man from the bushes, rob him, and kill him.

The story ends when Kausika dies, and he winds up in hell. He asks God, What in my saintly existence caused me to land in hell? God tells him, Your duty was to protect that man's life, and you didn't. The moral of the story is that mechanically following rules in the scriptures can put you into grave dilemmas. No matter what our faith, we need additional thought about the deeper issues of ethical behavior to make the right decision.

The next set of imperatives we consider from our religious touchstones are the positive ones. Religious guidance on the "shalls" is more diffuse and sometimes contradictory—especially if we follow rules loosely or we borrow principles from other faiths. These positive ethics can be thought of as a set of behaviors filling a periodic table of ethical elements. Our job is to decide which elements to call our own.

In the Qur'an, all manner of selflessness is urged. Charity is a common theme: "Treat with kindness your parents and kindred, and orphans and those in need; speak fair to the people; be steadfast in prayer; and practice regular charity."[7]

In Buddhism, positive ethics are often illustrated in one of the many stories about the Buddha in previous lives. One tells the tale of the Buddha-to-be in the form of a tortoise in the ocean. During a storm, a group of merchants struggle for their lives after a shipwreck. The giant tortoise saves the merchants by letting them climb on his back. He then swims to land, where, exhausted, he falls asleep with the merchants on the beach.[8]

The merchants, eventually awaking to their hunger and thirst, yearn for food. One of them suggests killing the tortoise. The tortoise overhears the desperate talk, yet he doesn't flee. Out of compassion, he decides to stay and let the merchants eat him. He sacrifices himself for the good of others.

Teachings of this selfless variety fill the Bible as well. During the Sermon on the Mount (Matthew 5–7), Jesus elaborates the Ten Commandments. He challenges his disciples: "But I say to you, do not resist one who is evil. But if any one strikes you on the right cheek, turn to him the other also; and if any one would sue you and take your coat, let him have your cloak as well; and if any one forces you to go one mile, go with him two miles. Give to him who begs from you, and do not refuse him who would borrow from you" (Matthew 5:39–42).

Of course, the question that comes up is this: How do mere mortals apply these lofty positive ethics to daily life? Jesus later describes (in Matthew 25:31–36) the positive ethic of those chosen for heaven: "I was hungry and you gave me food, I was thirsty and you gave me drink, I was a stranger and you welcomed me, I was naked and you clothed me, I was sick and you visited me, I was in prison and you came to me."

If we are like Mother Teresa of Calcutta, winner of the 1979 Nobel Peace Prize, we take Jesus's injunctions literally. She founded the now global, four thousand–nun Missionaries of Charity. She took in the poorest and sickest of mankind, from abandoned children to AIDS victims. For all intents and purposes, her mission echoed the words of Jesus: as expressed by one church leader, it was to care for "the hungry, the naked, the homeless, the crippled, the blind, the lepers, all those people who feel unwanted, unloved, uncared for throughout society, people that have become a burden to the society and are shunned by everyone."[9]

But, again, what does that mean for those of us living an ordinary day-to-day existence? If we turn to Buddhism, we get another round of guidance. Accepting the Nobel Peace Prize in 1989, the Dalai Lama,

leader of Tibetan Buddhism, gave a lecture that he ended with a favorite
prayer:

> *For as long as space endures,*
> *And for as long as living beings remain,*
> *Until then may I, too, abide*
> *To dispel the misery of the world.*[10]

So should we all take as our touchstone "to dispel the misery of the
world"? Even dispelling a small portion is a tall order. Such guidance can
leave us feeling adrift. Unfortunately, if we search in scripture for a description of just how positive we should be in daily life, we will be disap-
pointed. We seldom find hard-and-fast rules, with perhaps the exception
of references to tithing, defined as giving 10 percent of income to support
the clergy or church.

That's why we need to make another distinction, between positive
ethics and aspirations. In figuring out right from wrong, we seek to clarify
our positive ethics. In figuring out how we want to live, we will also think
about our aspirations. But clarifying our aspirations is not an ethical task,
even if ethical reflection spurs us to do so. And falling short of aspirations
is not unethical, even if we disappoint ourselves in the process.

So as we survey our touchstones, we will limit ourselves to the ethical
question, What does "right" behavior require? If we are compelled to consider a positive ethic, we realize we must eventually confront the issue of
drawing a line. How many of the homeless will we house? How many of the
naked will we clothe? How much misery in the world will we dispel? If we
review our religious upbringing, what does our inner voice tell us?

Across religions there emerges a useful rule of thumb: the Golden
Rule. Muslims may see it as "No one of you is a believer until he desires for
his brother that which he desires for himself" (Sunna. Forty Hadith of an-
Nawawi 13). Christians may see it as "Whatever you wish that men would
do to you, do so to them" (Matthew 7:12). Similar variations appear in
other religions.

A surprising insight comes to us when we look into the Golden Rule.
Like the statements of negative and positive religious-based ethics, it
doesn't always provide cut-and-dried guidance. At first we think the rule
shines a definitive guiding ethical light. But when we examine an issue

through the prism of ethical thinking, the light breaks into a spectrum of colors.

In our classes, we conduct an exercise to reveal this point—and to help everyone think about what the Golden Rule means to them. Partly in fun, we manufacture a selection of "metal rules," or Golden Rule variations. We then comment on the nature of each. The Golden Rule addresses the notion of reciprocity—putting ourselves in someone else's shoes. Using our prism, we see more colors of reciprocity than we had at first thought.

> **Golden Rule (restated as a positive ethic):** "Do unto others as you would have them do unto you." (Meaning in both positive and negative forms: *our* preferences govern how we treat others.)

> **Platinum Rule:** "Do unto others as they would have you do unto them." (Meaning: *others'* preferences govern how we treat them.)

> **Diamond Rule:** "Do unto others as the Buddha or Muhammad or Jesus (or your chosen venerated figure) would do unto you." (Meaning: our *aspirations* govern how we treat others.)

> **Silver Rule:** "Do not do unto others as you would not have them do unto you." (*Our* negative ethical preferences govern our behavior.)

> **Brass Rule:** "Do unto others as they do unto you." (*Others'* preferences govern our actions, good or bad.)

> **Aluminum Rule:** "Do not let others do to you what you would not do to them." (*Our* preferences for negative ethics govern preemptive behavior.)

> **Lead Rule:** "Undo others who undo you." (*Our temptation for retribution* trumps ethical behavior.)

> **Iron Rule:** "Do unto others before they do unto you." (*Our anticipation* of unethical behavior trumps ethical decisions.)

You can see the variety of thinking that gets tossed under the heading of the Golden Rule. And we could make up more rules—and you could do so on your own. The exercise has a way of making us laugh—laugh first because we realize we have all followed every one of the rules at some point, and laugh (perhaps nervously) because we realize how unclearly we have been thinking about the Golden Rule in the first place.

The metal rules also help us to realize some of the weaknesses of the Golden Rule.[11] It doesn't actually bar unethical acts by both sides. It doesn't define who the "other" is when the recipient of our behavior is not a specific person. And in religious scripture, the Golden Rule comes in many forms, some with different meanings.[12]

So we have to make some choices about what the Golden Rule means to us. We have to parse the words and decide what to embrace.

If we are Christians or Jews, we will know a closely related but different form of the Golden Rule, sometimes referred to as the royal law: "Love your neighbor as yourself" (Leviticus 19:18, Mark 12:31, James 2:8). When Jesus was asked which commandment was the first, he cited the royal law. (It was second only to the commandment to love God "with all your heart, and with all your soul, and with all your mind, and with all your strength" [Mark 12:28–31].)

If we were to follow the royal law, we would have to know what *love* means. In Corinthians 13:4–7, Paul tells us, "Love is patient and kind; love is not jealous or boastful; it is not arrogant or rude. Love does not insist on its own way; it is not irritable or resentful; it does not rejoice at wrong, but rejoices in the right. Love bears all things, believes all things, hopes all things, endures all things."

Again, a tall order. The royal law gives us some help, but its appeal to our aspirations sounds more fitting for weddings than for everyday life. We are left to struggle. The lesson: our religious touchstones simply don't offer an ethical algorithm to give us easy answers—or at least ones that are easy to live by. They aren't a perfectly polished touchstone to support clear decisions. We have to do some thinking ourselves. We have to reflect.

Our Secular Legacy

Next to religion, perhaps the most prominent strain of ethical guidance comes from our upbringing—from family, school, friends, community, and nation. When we look to these secular influences, the difficulty of coming up with solid personal principles actually becomes harder—and yet more important—because so many nuances and conflicts emerge.

Unlike religious touchstones, the touchstones from our secular life tend to have a more consequentialist strain. That's because during our growing years, we learn about ethics in practice. We see how others balance ethical principles with prudential concerns and, ironically, when they compromise themselves. In our secular upbringing, we face many choices about where to stick with the action-based approach and where to go with consequentialism—in other words, where we go with questionable means to justify beneficial ends.

If we listen to the voices of Moses, Buddha, Muhammad, and Jesus to establish ethical ideals from religion, we watch mothers, fathers, favorite teachers, founding fathers, mentors, and friends to shape our ethical practices in daily life. Consider, as an example of parental teaching, a passage from literature. In Shakespeare's *Hamlet*, the royal counselor Polonius gives advice to his son Laertes and finishes his classic speech as follows:

> *Give every man thy ear, but few thy voice;*
> *Take each man's censure, but reserve thy judgment.*
> *. . . Neither a borrower, nor a lender be;*
> *For loan oft loses both itself and friend,*
> *And borrowing dulls the edge of husbandry.*
> *This above all: to thine own self be true,*
> *And it must follow, as the night the day,*
> *Thou canst not then be false to any man.*[13]

Like many parents, Polonius gives his son absolutist ethical advice: "to thine own self be true." But he gives plenty of prudential pointers, too, in which he suggests Laertes weigh the consequences of his actions. Laertes may learn from religious touchstones to give the shirt off his back to help others, but from his father he learns never to lend anyone a nickel.

Such conflict is typical, and it comes up all the time during our upbringing. Parents say one thing and, if it suits their prudential interests, do another. Imagine for a moment the phone ringing in a modern-day household headed by Polonius. As young Laertes reaches for the handset, Polonius, tired from a long day of royal counseling, whispers, "If it's Prince Hamlet, tell him I'm not here." So much for being "true," Laertes thinks.

In spite of the conflicts in our upbringing, our first task, as with religious and philosophical touchstones, is to survey our secular touchstones for negative ethics. Many of them will be the same as religious ones, but there are exceptions. Today one big conflict, no matter our faith, is over the ethics of sex. Religions generally ban adultery and premarital sex. So we have to make an explicit decision of what kind of sexual behavior we consider right and wrong.

In our classes, students struggle with this one. To some students, fellatio is not sex. (Nor is it to some former presidents.) To others, such decisions are not ethical at all but merely prudential.

The behavior of friends and, more particularly, leaders of society will form another touchstone for ethical behavior. What echoes do we hear from those we admire that harmonize with our inner voice? As we look to great men and women, we can usually steer clear of princes, presidents, and politicians. We find more ethical examples in the likes of Albert Einstein, Nelson Mandela, and Mohandas Gandhi.

Gandhi, arguably the most influential ethical leader of the twentieth century, inspired others around the world with his ethical conduct. When violence flared during the independence movement in India, he stood firm for nonviolence. In 1919, British troops massacred at least 379 Indian civilians in Jallianwala Bagh, a town square in Punjab. The slaughter ended only when troops fired 1,600 rounds and ran out of ammunition. Indian reaction was violent; at least 5 Europeans were killed. Gandhi pleaded for restraint, saying Indians should not take revenge but instead work to change the system. His acts of nonviolent resistance (*satyagraha*) became models for other leaders like Martin Luther King.[14]

On a more modest level, we can find notable role models among even sports figures. At the time in 1990 when University of Colorado football coach Bill McCartney claimed victory over Missouri in spite of winning on a mistaken fifth down, sports writers turned up a better role model.[15] In 1940, in a football game between Cornell and Dartmouth, Cornell won the game with a touchdown pass on another infamous mistaken fifth down. After reviewing game film over the next two days, Cornell's coach and athletic director recognized the error. They forfeited the game by telegram: "Cornell relinquishes claim to the victory and extends congratulations to Dartmouth."[16]

Schools provide added material for ethical touchstones. Many, like Stanford University, have codes that focus on plagiarism and cheating. Favorite teachers, professors, and coursework from school years often offer yet more material. In the 1980s, a student at Grinnell College in Iowa, while preparing a paper on Fyodor Dostoevsky's *Brothers Karamazov*, copied two clever ideas advanced by a pair of Dostoevsky experts without giving appropriate attribution. The professor readily noticed the theft, and he sat the student down to talk about the evils of plagiarism. The professor could have failed the student or expelled him from class. Instead, he explained how the student was cheating both himself and others. That student, an author of this book, will take that experience to his grave.

One honor code that provides a useful benchmark for school-based touchstones is the code at West Point, the U.S. Military Academy. The Spartan and blunt wording of the code, now famous, is sandblasted into polished granite on the school campus: "A cadet will not lie, cheat, steal, or tolerate those who do."[17]

The code is noteworthy, but not for its rigidity. Nor for how well it works, since in the 1970s, 150 cadets were caught cheating on a take-home exam, an episode that still haunts the academy. It's noteworthy instead because of the way the military academy thoughtfully defines what various terms mean.

Lying has an unambiguous meaning. One part of the definition is to "deliberately deceive another person by stating an untruth, or by any direct form of communication, to include the telling of a partial truth or the vague or ambiguous use of information or language, with the intent to deceive or mislead."

Another part addresses equivocation: "To equivocate or 'quibble' is to use deliberately vague, misleading, or ambiguous language. Equivocation usually occurs when a cadet tells a literal truth which he knows will mislead another person, when a person tells a 'half-truth,' or when a person attempts to avoid the act of telling an untruth by making vague statements with the intent to mislead another."

The code is similarly specific about theft: "Stealing does not require the possession of tangible objects. Obtaining a service without permission or payment constitutes stealing. Shorting an arcade machine to get a free game, tapping into TV cable . . . sneaking into movies, and using someone else's phone card and pin number without permission are examples of service theft."

And borrowing can be theft, too: "Improper borrowing occurs when a cadet takes another cadet's property with the intention of returning it, but without prior verbal or written permission, or fails to return it in a manner and condition satisfactory to the owner."

The West Point code strikes many as exacting. Indeed, a cadet prayer evokes the high-mindedness: "Make us to choose the harder right instead of the easier wrong and never to be content with a half-truth when the whole can be won." But the code provides a clear standard useful as we clarify our negative ethics.

While weighing our secular upbringing, we will also want to look for positive ethics. Parents, leaders, and schools all provide helpful models as touchstones. When Nelson Mandela was released from twenty-seven years in prison in 1990, he expressed no bitterness, exacted no retribution. His positive ethic of reconciliation instead forestalled civil war. He once said, "Our talking with the enemy was a domination of the brain over emotion, without which our country would have turned into rivers of blood."[18]

For a young United States of America, Benjamin Franklin was a source of positive ethics. Franklin created and revealed in his autobiography a system of practicing thirteen virtues, which included a mixture of positive ethics, negative ethics, and prudential rules. Among them: temperance ("drink not to elevation"), sincerity ("[speak] innocently and justly"), moderation ("forbear resenting injuries"), humility ("Imitate Jesus and Socrates"), and chastity ("Rarely use venery but for health or offspring"). Franklin even kept a daily pocket ledger, keeping track of backsliding and weaknesses by category.[19]

Yet other elements from our upbringing that are useful as ethical touchstones include values expressed by civic institutions. At the grassroots level, there are youth groups, like Boy Scouts or Girl Scouts, with their scout laws and promises. (The emphasis on loyalty and obedience, as we saw in the last chapter, has questionable ethical value.) At the global level, we may view the values of the United Nations, codified in many documents, as useful. The Universal Declaration of Human Rights, now more than fifty years old, gives a formulation of the Golden Rule: "All human beings . . . should act towards one another in a spirit of brotherhood."[20]

Do our secular touchstones provide much perspective on the Golden Rule? As a touchstone, the West Point code again provides useful material. The West Point ethics system includes "Three Rules of Thumb."[21] The rules, or more accurately questions, essentially define the Golden Rule.

If a cadet can answer no to all three questions, an action passes muster:

a. Does this action attempt to deceive anyone or allow anyone to be deceived?

b. Does this action gain or allow the gain of privilege or advantage to which I or someone else would not otherwise be entitled?

c. Would I be dissatisfied by the outcome if I were on the receiving end of this action?

We would all find it useful to similarly articulate our own statement of reciprocity.

Our Work Legacy

After religious and secular touchstones, the most important in our lives are touchstones from the work world. What is the policy, and how do people behave? What is expected in our profession?

Many years ago, the chief executive officer of an auto-parts company was faced with a painful decision in Taiwan. To get shipments off the dock and onto a ship bound for the United States and Canada, longshoremen required small bribes, so-called facilitating payments, of roughly $40. The CEO couldn't stomach the idea, and it was against company policy, but he couldn't see a way around it. He decided to compromise. Rather than hiding the bribes, he authorized them so long as they were openly accounted for monthly.[22]

"We said we'd compromise our principles, but we're going to compromise above the board and not below the board," the CEO said. He admitted he committed a wrong, but he refused to label it a right. At least this CEO was honest with himself.

Stories like these fuel the theory that work and private ethics are different. We don't agree. Work and private *temptations* may be different. Prudential pressures like the cost of failing to get shipments off the dock in Asia may seem to put decisions in a different light. But we have to account to the same conscience for whatever we do. Our inner voice sticks with us wherever we are. Rationalizations paint over ethical errors today, but when the paint chips, all becomes visible, and the fallout costly.

That's why most companies today have strict and detailed ethics codes. These codes commit employees to the high road, detailing both negative and positive ethics. Like documents from the Business Round-table, International Chamber of Commerce, or OECD (Organisation for Economic Cooperation and Development), such codes can provide help-ful touchstones for our personal codes. (On the other hand, if the codes have provisions like "we shall not speak ill of a competitive product," they can create conflicts with truth telling.)

But the behavior of individual managers in the end ranks higher as an influential ethical touchstone than written codes. We can hope the auto-parts executive's other actions reaffirmed what he stood for. In the re-search for this book, a dentist complained about patients who asked him to alter his diagnoses to boost insurance reimbursements. The dentist found the request distasteful, saying, "If I was willing to cheat the insur-ance company, what makes you think I wouldn't cheat you?"

At least as important as company-sponsored ethics statements are those sponsored by professional organizations. Professional codes have extensive and high-minded negative and positive ethics. They stress dis-closure, candor, client confidentiality, truthfulness, and a total lack of de-ceit. They insist on fulfilling one's duty to society and the profession, and taking responsibility for continually improving professional skills. They are an essential complement to other touchstones.

Each professional code deals with particularities of the profession and in that way provides unique guidance. In the code for coaches of the U.S. Olympic Committee, one prominent issue is the risk of exploitative rela-tionships. Thus reads one section, "Coaches do not engage in sexual/ro-mantic relationships with athletes or other participants over whom the coach has evaluative, direct, or indirect authority, because such relation-ships are likely to impair judgment or be exploitative."[23]

The code of the American Medical Association addresses an issue of similar importance to physicians: "The patient's right of self-decision can be effectively exercised only if the patient possesses enough information to enable an informed choice. The patient should make his or her own determination on treatment. The physician's obligation is to present the medical facts . . . Informed consent is a basic policy in both ethics and law that physicians must honor."[24]

The issue of client confidentiality comes up often in the professions, especially law. The American Bar Association's Model Rules for Professional Conduct forbid revealing information without the client's consent. Still, lawyers may reveal information if they believe it will "prevent certain death or substantial bodily harm . . . prevent the client from committing a [substantial] crime or fraud . . . prevent, mitigate, or rectify substantial injury to the financial interest or property of another."[25]

Today nearly every profession has an ethics code. It is true that in the daily news, we get the impression many working people ignore them. But inspiring stories from work emerge all the time, and across history. Another historical example is an incident from the 1820s that offers a direct parallel to the story of the tortoise (Buddha) sacrificing himself for the merchants. On the search for sperm whales in the Pacific Ocean, the Nantucket whaling ship *Essex* went down at sea after a rogue sperm whale rammed it. The ship's crew, adrift at sea in three whale-hunting rowboats, saved itself only through cannibalism.

Re-creating this unique story, author Nathaniel Philbrick recounts how at one point the surviving sailors, adrift for more than two months, chose not to starve to death together.[26] They agreed instead to draw lots, and the unlucky man would allow the others to kill him for food. In essence, his death was an act of self-sacrifice, the ultimate act of compassion, recognized by everyone in advance.

Though it's a grisly story, there is no ethical dilemma here. The killing and cannibalism were premeditated prudential acts, not ethical ones. Of the twenty-one crewmen, eight survived, rescued over three months after their ship sank.

Miscues of the Rich and Famous

Once we survey religious, secular, and work touchstones, we have an ample base for making decisions about our own ethical code. As we take stock of the available guidance, we need to beware of false touchstones. As we learned in chapter 1, even Abraham Lincoln sometimes did not offer a model we could call a touchstone, however much he may have believed his contradictory statements.

Lincoln was responsible for publicizing the mistruths of another president, however. When he was a young congressman, in the 1840s, he listened as President James K. Polk championed the doctrine of Manifest Destiny.[27] Polk stretched the truth to serve his vision of a nation extending from the Atlantic to the Pacific. In a speech before Congress in 1846, he told lawmakers the Mexican Army had crossed into the United States and "shed American blood upon the American soil."

This wasn't true; Mexican soldiers had killed U.S. soldiers, but in contested territory. Polk's story gave him the excuse to incite Congress to declare war against Mexico. Lincoln, outraged throughout the ensuing Mexican-American War, challenged Polk from the start: "Show me the spot" on U.S. soil where American blood was shed, Lincoln reportedly demanded.[28]

If we are to look to "great leaders" for touchstone material, we learn an old lesson: popularity is no indicator of character. Leaders sometimes follow the old adage "Don't let the facts get in the way of a good story." And that goes for leaders from all walks of life.

In another case, the Church of England long condoned slavery. The owner of the 710-acre Codrington sugar plantation in Barbados was the church itself, and so the church had a prudential interest in seeing slavery persist. The English at the time had a keen understanding that slaves were property—the word *society* (a reference to the church operation) was burned into the chests of the church's slaves.[29] Apparently, the taking of property was recognized as anathema, while the taking of freedom was not.

In a revealing footnote in history, as abolitionist fever roiled England in the late 1700s, the United States' soon-to-be-president George Washington remained a committed slave owner. He met in New York with a British commander in 1783 after the British defeat in the American Revolution. The number one item on his agenda was getting Britain to return property, above all slaves, including Washington's. Washington actually carried a long list of runaway slave names with him.

It wasn't Washington's behavior that became a touchstone in this case; it was the conduct of British commander Sir Guy Carleton. The slaves had defected to the British side during the war to take advantage of a British policy of giving slaves freedom. Though representing a defeated power,

Sir Guy refused Washington's insistence that he renege on the British promise. Sir Guy had the audacity to insist the three thousand slaves encamped with the British in New York remain free—and he prevailed.[30]

In spite of leaders like Sir Guy, false idols are everywhere. In 1993, basketball star Charles Barkley ran in a series of Nike advertisements with the comment "I am not a role model." Many agreed, but athletes like Barkley are role models nonetheless, owing to their fame, riches, and success. Barkley became a sports antihero, a bad-boy role model, known for blunt commentary and impulsive behavior like spitting on a girl at courtside.[31] He set a certain tawdry standard, easily copied.

In a story reprising the themes of the University of Colorado football incident, U.S. gymnast Paul Hamm won a contested gold medal in the 2004 Olympic Games in Athens. After Hamm accepted the medal, a calculation error was discovered. He didn't win after all; South Korean Yang Tae Young did. In an embarrassing effort to right the wrong, the head of the International Gymnastics Federation suggested Hamm give the medal to the genuine winner.[32] Hamm refused. Hamm recognized the error but argued that scorings could not be contested after competitions end.

Hamm was right about the rules. After a final appeal was heard, the Court of Arbitration for Sport in Lausanne, Switzerland, ruled in his favor, and Hamm kept the medal. The October 2004 decision was based on legal grounds, of course, which served Hamm's and the U.S. Olympic Committee's prudential interests. Judges took no position on the ethical dimension of the decision, a fact many observers seemed to miss. Hamm's behavior thus makes for poor material as an ethical touchstone.

Mimicking the lifestyle of the rich and famous, as portrayed in myth, legend, and reality, is seductive. Unfortunately, it often provides a model of behavior exemplifying principles like "Might makes right," or "Possession is half the law," or "Honesty equals popularity," or "Don't let the facts get in the way of a good story." So when we search for touchstones on which to base our ethical codes, we need to remain ever wary of false idols.

Reconciling the Touchstones

After pondering ethical touchstones from our religious, secular, and work lives, we come to several realizations. First, we have scanned many layers

of ethical guidance. From the bedrock of religious and philosophical prohibitions to the layers of principles laid down by our parents, to the gems
collected in daily experience, we have amassed a whole geology of ethical
thinking. We realize that in this geology we already have a nascent ethical
code. It contains a number of high-level principles that are the foundation
of our ethical preferences.

We also realize that this examination gets us only so far. If we were
born with the emotional, intellectual, and spiritual intelligence of a Jesus
Christ or Siddhartha Gautama Buddha, we would not need to take our
ethical reflection further. In fact, we wouldn't need to undertake it at all.
And if we were gifted decision makers, the likes of a Nelson Mandela, we
could make wise ethical choices with just the principles.

But most of us realize the signals from our touchstones have limitations. They don't always provide guidance that's clear. They don't offer
rules that are complete for day-to-day living. And they come handed to us
by others, echoing ethical strains from other people's inner voices. We
have not actually thought through our unique principles to find those that
inspire us.

To continue to lay the groundwork for becoming skillful ethical decision makers, we each need to refine and vet the signals from the touchstones. As Aleksandr Solzhenitsyn said, "The line separating good and evil
passes . . . right through every human heart—and through all human
hearts."[33] We have to define the precise location of that line ourselves.

Think back to Ali Hasan. The Qur'an instructed him and all Muslims
to be good to the near of kin. Did that mean hiring relatives in preference to
people with better qualifications? The Golden Rule instructed him to give
to his brother as to himself. Did that mean, narrowly, to kin and friends, or
broadly, to all company employees, all candidates in the applicant pool,
or all engineers in the profession at large?

Hasan recognized that he had to draw the line. He also realized that
such decisions remain challenging for each and every one of us—even as
we do draw the line. Of his view toward nepotism today, he said, "I do not
plan to do it, but I know it is very hard to fight the whole family when it
comes to situations where you can help and you do not."

Hasan quotes a famous Islamic Hadith as inspiration: "When asked,
'What is the major jihad?' the Prophet replied: 'The jihad of the self'

(struggle against self)."[34] And that is the struggle we continue in the next chapter.

➤ Your Turn: Outline Your Principles

Now that you've taken a mental trip across the landscape of your ethical and moral touchstones, it is time to commit your principles to paper. What are the half-dozen principles your inner voice tells you to hold dear? For simplicity, start with principles for deception, stealing, and harming. Identify, as a further aid, your top one or two ethical role models. What principles do you think they hold dear? For a list of potential tochstones, see the chapter 3 notes starting on page 194 and www.ethicsfortherealworld .com.

CHAPTER 4

Draft Your Code

Committing Yourself to Ethical Principles

*The moral virtues, then, are produced in us neither
by nature nor against nature. Nature, indeed,
prepares in us the ground for their reception, but
their complete formation is the product of habit.*

—Aristotle[1]

Y EARS AGO, the head of a local law firm was shopping at a
yard sale held by a woman recently widowed. He came across
a legal briefcase, almost unused, recently the property of the widow's husband. The briefcase, easily worth $300, was selling for $40. He said to the
widow, "Don't you realize how much this is worth?" She answered discon-
solately, "I don't care; I just want to get rid of it."

The attorney paid the $40 and walked away. But he never used the
briefcase. Instead of becoming a valued possession, it reminded him more
and more of what he felt was an impropriety—profiting from a widow's anguish—even though he never violated any ethical principle.

Or did he?

The question of an ethical violation is not something we could answer for the attorney. And the answer was not something he could draw from the high-level principles we identified in the last chapter—from the Ten Commandments, the echoes of parental edicts, or the examples of admired leaders and mentors. The circumstances of the briefcase bargain raised an issue not covered in these touchstones. It was an issue the attorney had not thought about, and it made him uncomfortable, no matter the typical rules of commerce.

In situations of this kind—whether about trivial yard-sale ethics or life-changing ethics about abortion or assisted suicide—reliance on traditional ethical touchstones often falls short. Yes, the touchstones' guidance is necessary for recognizing our core principles. No, it is not sufficient for skillful ethical decision making. We have to supplement with the subtler utterances of our inner voice. We have to find answers through additional reflection.

Consider other ethical areas that could spur remorse. If we acquire a sofa with a thirty-day money-back guarantee with no intention of keeping it, will we feel uncomfortable that we took something that did not seem like ours? If we are a drug researcher who benefits from data obtained from experiments on unwilling prisoners, will we feel we have encouraged harm of other prisoners in the future? If we work for a firm that extracts oil (or nickel or timber) from an underdeveloped country where the military relocates people to make way for our operations, will we suffer from guilt over theft or harm perpetrated by the military on our watch?

The best time to answer these questions is before we face them. We can then consider, without the distorting pressures of a real situation, how they affect our character and relationships. The lesson is that we have to fill the gaps left by our touchstones. We need to develop our own detailed guidance. We need to create a personal code—an ethical guide for the real world.

To write our ethical code, we will follow a simple step-by-step process. We start by documenting our thinking from the last chapter, where we explored our own ethical consciences. We will then continue with our self-discovery process to identify a variety of situations we personally feel are ethically sensitive, to create a tool to decide how to handle them, and to learn to build character and strengthen relationships by developing good ethical habits.

In the process, we discover that the benefits of a personal code go beyond the guidance of the core principles. Even when the principles seem to suffice, their wisdom falls short for skillful decision making because the advice was developed by somebody else. We often don't feel personally invested in it. By creating our own code, we can commit to guidance we believe in. We can come up with principles and rules we really mean, rather than simply saying we agree with others.

A code thought out beforehand would have helped our attorney friend. He had thought he bought the bargain briefcase with a clear conscience: he was honest with the widow and used no deception. But in hindsight he felt queasy—apparently about an ethical distinction that was important to him, if not others. The lesson is that we need to listen to— and if needed, educate—our inner voice on our personal rules for ethical behavior.

Our colleague had never thought through the concept of profiting from another's misfortune. If he had, he could have identified it as one of his personal sensitivities, acted accordingly, and avoided the remorse. The next time he faces that concept, his experience will be a reminder, and he will be more prepared to act.

The Ethical Code Process

A successful code helps you clarify for yourself your ethical principles. It helps you resist temptations, especially those most relevant to you, your profession, your weaknesses, and your aspirations. It can be as short as a few sentences, or as long as many pages. We present here a three-step process, but beware of simply copying our issues and language. This is your code; it must work for you. It should inspire you to think.

The three steps we follow to write our code are (1) drafting standards, (2) testing standards, and (3) refining the code to make it practical. While we don't need to do the steps in order, each one adds to a more thoughtful code—and lays the basis for more skillful decision making.

Step 1: Drafting Standards

To get started with our code, the easiest approach is to focus on the three principal categories of ethical wrongdoing: deceiving, stealing, and harming.

We have almost certainly thought through each of these issues while reading chapter 3. Experience shows that, no matter what our religion or culture, we will consider these three central to ethical behavior. It is now time to investigate the nuances.

As in the briefcase example, the nuances can pose significant thinking challenges. Small things, no less than the big ones, reveal unresolved conflicts. In fact, the big ethical topics of the day often figure far less into our daily lives than a host of small persnickety ones.

To speed our reflection, see table 4-1, which begins with three categorically stated negative ethics: "Lying and deceiving are wrong," "Stealing is wrong," and "Harming is wrong." We can identify the nuances in our ethical thinking simply by choosing exceptions to each of these statements. That is, which of these exceptions feel right? Which ones affect other people in ways we consider acceptable?

The issue that figures most prominently in our daily lives is usually deception. So to investigate nuances to "Lying and deception are wrong," it helps to reflect on real-world situations that invoke such exceptions. Recall, for example, the vignettes in earlier chapters: Lowballing the estimate of a project's cost. Overstating revenue projections for a high-tech start-up. Billing two clients for the same travel time. Signing off on deceptive financial statements. Which of these are ethically acceptable, or have acceptable consequences on relationships with others?

We learn quickly in this short exercise that relying solely on high-level principles may not offer enough guidance. We realize that questions like When would you not tell the whole truth? can't be answered on reflex. We need to think back to times when we did not act in line with our high-level principles, times that we regret. And we need to think forward, using table 4-1, to anticipate when our principles might not apply.

Once we have considered the fundamental issues of deceiving, stealing, and harming, we can add to the list. It would be a mistake to list every ethical question that comes to mind, of course. Shorter codes are more effective codes. But we will want to identify the unique temptations in our own lives. Note which ethical compromises seduce us most persistently—and leave a legacy of remorse. Which leave our inner voice stammering for clarity on what's right and wrong?

TABLE 4-1

Drafting your ethical code

What exceptions will you accept?

Lying/deception	Stealing	Harming
Lying and deceiving are wrong, except for: (check all that apply)	*Stealing is wrong, except for:* (check all that apply)	*Harming is wrong, except for:* (check all that apply)

Lying/deception

Lying and deceiving are wrong, except for:
(check all that apply)

☐ Telling lies to save someone's feelings

☐ Telling lies to avoid embarrassment

☐ Telling lies to avoid punishment

☐ Telling lies to get ahead

☐ Inflating qualifications on a resume

☐ Exaggerating benefits/ hiding deficiencies to a customer

☐ Telling lies in negotiation

☐ Telling "white" lies

☐ Telling lies to liars

☐ Telling lies to children

☐ Telling lies to your parents

☐ Telling lies to competitors

☐ Telling lies to protect property

☐ Telling lies to prevent harm to self or others

☐ Using euphemistic language

☐ Making promises I do not intend to keep

☐ Giving false impressions through nonverbal means

☐ Not correcting misimpressions

☐ Cheating when "everyone else is doing it"

☐ _____

☐ _____

☐ *Check if no exceptions*

Key question:

When would I not tell the whole truth?

Stealing

Stealing is wrong, except for:
(check all that apply)

☐ Stealing when it is easy and I won't get caught

☐ Stealing to get ahead

☐ Stealing to help others

☐ Stealing office supplies

☐ Inflating billable hours

☐ Copying copyrighted print matter

☐ Copying/downloading software

☐ Copying/downloading music

☐ Copying/downloading movies

☐ Borrowing without permission

☐ Stealing from thieves

☐ Stealing from rich people

☐ Stealing from big organizations

☐ Stealing from anonymous victims

☐ Stealing if you think the owner will not miss it

☐ Profiting from others' ignorance

☐ Profiting from others' billing mistakes

☐ Stealing when "everyone else is doing it"

☐ _____

☐ _____

☐ *Check if no exceptions*

Key question:

When would I take another's property without asking for permission?

Harming

Harming is wrong, except for:
(check all that apply)

☐ Harming in self-defense

☐ Harming to defend others

☐ Harming those who have harmed others

☐ Threatening to harm

☐ Inciting violence to make a political point

☐ Imposing undisclosed risks on friends

☐ Going to work when contagious with the flu

☐ Not telling a sexual partner you have a sexually transmitted disease

☐ Imposing undisclosed risks on strangers

☐ Driving while intoxicated

☐ Working for an organization that harms innocent people

☐ Patronizing or investing in an organization that harms innocent people

☐ Assisting suicide

☐ Harming when "everyone else is doing it"

☐ Working for an organization whose products harm innocent people

☐ _____

☐ _____

☐ *Check if no exceptions*

Key question:

How close to others committing harm is too close for me?

Do we feel remorseful for not reporting an incompetent legal or medical colleague? Are we torn by benefiting from research that uses embryonic stem cells? In an example from one of our classes, an undergraduate student was preoccupied with issues of romantic relationships—keeping secrets, revealing affairs, expressing opinions. An older student was focused on issues from work—conflicts of interest, data manipulation, gift giving, excess reimbursement, insider information.

Although we should err on the side of broad principles, we should not omit the big questions in our lives. Other common big issues include secrets (When will we agree to keep one, and reveal one?); promises (When will we make one, and break one?); influences (When will we bribe, use favoritism, or accept a conflict of interest?); sexual behavior (When will we consent to romantic activity, to sex outside a committed relationship, or to not informing a partner about transmitted diseases?); and reproductive behavior (When will we accept birth control, abortion, surrogate parenting, or egg/sperm donation?).

Remember, our choices of ethical issues, and the exceptions to standards, stem from the particularities of our inner voice, not someone else's. The concept of profiting from misfortune will seem silly to some people. But whether others feel our topics are silly or not, when we get up in the morning, we each have to look in our own ethical mirror. The question is not whether a briefcase-buying professor we observed on Saturday was right or wrong—we may feel his actions comport well with the unwritten rules of yard sales—but whether we have thought deeply enough to identify nuanced ethical issues for ourselves.

One of our student's exceptions to truth telling illustrates this: "I will lie, mislead, tell a partial truth, or offer a bribe for these reasons: (a) to save my life or the life of someone I care about; (b) to prevent myself or someone I care about from suffering due to another person's cruelty; (c) to give someone moral support as long as that person knows precisely what I am not being honest about, has heard the whole truth from me before, and desires in this instance to be lied to." These exceptions demonstrate the typical starting place for many of our students. As our students think more deeply about the implications of their codes, exceptions such as *b* and *c* tend to appear less often.

In spite of our touchstones, the standards we later draft for our code may sometimes clash with them. When this happens, we will need to resolve the conflict explicitly. One of our students is a Jain, a member of an ancient religion of India. He struggled with a conflict over assisted suicide, an anathema in Jainism. His resolution: "I would authorize, aid, and actively support an assisted suicide if it were the expressed interest of the patient or the patient gave any indication whatsoever that he/she wanted to commit suicide. I believe that if it is the expressed desire of the patient to die at a certain stage in their disease development, this wish should be respected—and I would help carry it out. Although Jainism may look down upon this, it also holds great respect for others' wishes and beliefs. Hence, this may be considered as having respect for another's autonomy."

Here again, codes often read in this fashion to begin with. Later steps in refining the code, or later iterations of the code, usually lead people to simplify the ethical principles. Note how the first sentence seems to open the door to euthanasia under "any indication whatsoever." Later refinements of the code will likely lead to more precise language.

Step 2: Testing the Code

How do we know our code is worthwhile? Is it academic theory or a practical tool? Several tests help us find out:

- **Check the logic.** Will our standards hold up to tests for reciprocity and universality?

- **Check for focus.** Have we included too many ethical statements, making the code unmanageable?

- **Test-drive for usefulness.** How well do our standards operate in everyday life? Are they practical? Do we really mean them?

CHECK THE LOGIC. Two principles of logic guide the construction of durable, thoughtful codes. The first is universality. The second is reciprocity. When we draft an ethical standard, we should ask, "Would I want everyone to follow this?" And "Would I want other people applying the same rule to me?" We need to shift our perspective in the same way we would with the Golden Rule—to a person in another set of shoes.

Consider the issue of telling the truth. Say our principle is, "I will tell the truth at all times." Would we want everyone to follow this rule? Would we want others applying it to us? In this case, the answer is yes. The two logic tests hold. Adhering to universality and reciprocity does not rule out exceptions, so long as the exceptions also fit the two rules. For example, we could select the exception of lying in self-defense.

Consider another issue: copying proprietary content on the Internet. Say our principle is, "I will not steal copyrighted property, except for works available for downloading on the Web." Many people take just this kind of laissez-faire approach to downloading (without payment) copyrighted music, software, and videos. Entire music libraries are built daily from copyrighted media downloaded without permission.

But the ethical questions to ask are plain: Would universal copying of music, software, and video make a sensible exception to the ethic of refraining from theft? If I were the author, composer, or musician, would I have the same view? Would I be happy to allow free copying of music, software, or videos I produced as part of my livelihood? Even if we initially judge downloading harmless and (therefore) ethical, tests for universality and reciprocity may change our minds.

A good idea at this point is to refer back to a couple of the tests in chapter 2: the other-shoe test, the role-model test, and the loved-one test. If we put ourselves in the position of another—a friend, a role model, a loved one—would our judgment about reciprocity change? For example, what would our mother think? These tests keep the focus on the effects of our ethical decisions on others.

CHECK FOR FOCUS. We should test to be sure we have winnowed the list of ethical topics to a manageable number. Scores, sometimes hundreds, of items populate our ethical thinking. We need to cut the list to a dozen or two by dropping unimportant ones—the least bothersome, unlikely to happen, or most trivial.

That isn't to suggest leaving out any burning issues, even if they seem trivial to other people. A construction manager's code, for example, includes unique work standards. He admits that clients will never know if workers dump cigarette butts or litter into reinforced concrete unless the contractor discloses the fact. He then commits to disclosing such lapses—and fixing them—even if it costs his company money.

This same manager has a second rule about lying. He commits to admitting his faults. He notes that some project managers attribute their own faults to mistakes by designers, clients, or even their subordinates. They do so to avoid losing their clients' trust. But in keeping with his ethical standard of not telling a lie, he will take responsibility for his errors.

We need meanwhile to eliminate prudential issues. Although prudential issues play a huge part in our lives, they should play no part in our codes. Delete phrases like the following: "I will be an informed citizen of my country, assess government policies for myself, and take a position on international developments." Also cull statements like, "I will keep my perspective on work-family balance; I won't forget life's more important issues, including faith, culture, constant learning, and compassion."

Other prudential statements, equally laudable, give similarly ambiguous guidance for ethical action. They should be cut:

I will treat others with respect.

I will be accountable for my actions.

I will not discriminate.

I will actively seek out knowledge.

I will balance work and family life.

I will accept and process constructive criticism.

I will minimize gossiping and hurtful talk.

The word *respect* appears in many codes. Its appearance, however, should be a red flag, as it gives ambiguous guidance. Does it suggest we tell white lies to spare others' feelings? Or tell the truth to help people see themselves for what they are? Or categorize ill-mannered or contemptuous behavior as unethical? If we use *respect*, we need to specify the related behaviors that would be right or wrong.

As we winnow our list, we will find it useful to pare the positive ethics. Generally, positive ethics respond to an almost unlimited range of altruistic ambitions. On the modest side, we may add positive ethics to lying, stealing, and harming—namely to foster truth, restore stolen property, and help people avoid harm. On the ambitious side, we may include any number of high-minded statements, as the Dalai Lama and Mother Teresa would.

The difficulty with positive ethics is they know no bounds. We could never honor our entire list of altruistic intentions as ethical standards, or we wouldn't have time to do anything else. So we need to make choices. Many people leave positive ethics out of their codes altogether. Other people include a couple—for example, statements related to charity (giving to others rather than taking) and compassion (helping others rather than harming).

TEST-DRIVE FOR USEFULNESS. A third test is to reconsider our codes for usefulness: are they practical? Many people settle with codes that prescribe behavior short of their ideals precisely because they know they cannot put their ideals into action. Committing to a code we can keep is far better than committing to one that stretches us too far, forcing us to break our own rules.

The practical problem comes when an overly strict code tempts us into compromising on just one item, but the compromise calls into question the usefulness of the whole code. While it is a good idea to challenge ourselves to improve our ethical performance, we need to calibrate the code so we can win the next time we face temptation. When we are testing our codes, we ask, "Do I really mean what I wrote?"

A week-kneed code is not helpful either. One code reads, "I believe that honesty is the best policy, and [I should] tell it like it is. At the same time . . . I cannot adopt a positive ethic to tell the truth. Omission sometimes saves both host and guest." This code opens the door to white lies.

The same is true of the following: "If the consequences of a lie are minor (negative or positive), I reserve the right to lie . . . If the entire family is gathered around the Christmas tree, and Grandma asks me if I like the purple slippers she knit for me, I reserve the right to say yes."

The test for usefulness is crucial when our code includes positive ethics. Negative ethics often take little or no energy to execute. That is, we don't come home from a long day at work exhausted by resisting the temptation to lie, steal, and harm. In contrast, we easily exhaust ourselves with positive ethics. They may violate what we call the *energy rule*, which means that we all have a limited supply of positive energy.

One code that puts the writer at risk of code violations from the start has six positive ethics, which commit the person to "Financially helping the poor . . . Giving advice to others as needed . . . Stopping people from hurting themselves and others . . . Helping others with their important educational decisions." These are worthy goals but probably unrealistic ethics.

If we have a lot of positive ethics, we will find that in daily life we have to balance them, trading one off for the other. For a consequence-based ethical decision maker, writing a code requiring ethical trade-offs is in keeping with standard operating procedure, even if this procedure can tie decision making in knots. But for an action-based thinker, trade-offs are unworkable.

If we run a few scenarios in our minds, we can quickly reveal whether our code works in the roles and settings we typically encounter in our lives. Starting at home, does the code apply to our behavior toward spouses, partners, children, and other loved ones? Ask, "Do I want my children to follow my example?"

Say we draft the standard "I cannot adopt a positive ethic to tell the truth. Omission sometimes saves both host and guest." Imagine a situation in which we are too tired to go to a party. We decide to phone our hosts the next morning to say we were ill. Are we comfortable making a habit of that behavior among people we know? What effect does using white lies to excuse social lapses have on relationships?

Another question we may ask is, "What if my behavior received publicity?" It might enter the rumor mill, or become the subject of stories around the water cooler. Or for more serious transgressions, we could ask, "Would I be happy if my actions were reported in the local paper?" We can borrow the front-page test (and other tests) from chapter 2 and force ourselves to see our actions as if they are transparent to a world of others. The specter of publicity often changes our viewpoint.

Another tactic that creates fresh perspective is imagining a different person on the receiving end of our actions. Would we act the same with our boss, our spouse, our children, our neighbors? What if the person is ambiguous or anonymous? Suppose the "person" is the corporate owner of a broken vending machine that dispenses free snacks? Or what if the person is someone we dislike, or someone who is angry or dishonest or rude or incompetent or a thief? Do our principles and rules still make sense?

We can employ thought experiments to test extremes. Say we drafted a principle that we will never kill. We then ask, Would we kill someone if our spouse asked? Probably not. Would we kill for $1 million? Probably not. Would we kill if transplanting the person's liver would save two other people? Would we kill if the person's liver contained a substance to cure cancer?

If we are a consequentialist, we face many difficult questions of this kind. We need to subject our codes to simulations to decide whether we want to reengineer them. If our codes work, we expect them to provide a basis for skillful ethical decision making, and in turn better our lives in concrete ways, improving character and strengthening relationships. Have we produced a tool that does so?

Step 3: Refining the Code

The tests lead us to refining the code. We stress three ways to do so:

- **Clarify degrees of separation.** Can we more explicitly specify "how close is too close" to unethical action?

- **Draw sharper lines.** Can we draw clearer lines for our positive ethics?

- **Consider a hierarchy.** If two or more ethics conflict, which ones get priority?

CLARIFY DEGREES OF SEPARATION. Every code needs to contain an answer to the question, How close is too close? Even when we don't occupy a position to take unethical action, our family, company, organization, government, and other associations connect us to many ethically debatable acts. If we are an indirect party to these acts, for which ones do we share culpability?

There is no stock answer. Say we volunteer at a homeless shelter. We are committed to our work, and we find it gratifying. But we discover the director inflates client numbers to extract better funding from agencies and local philanthropies. Are we working too closely with a liar to stay on?

Or say we consider the sale of tobacco products wrong, because we believe it violates an ethic of not harming others. Is it then ethical to work on a tobacco farm? How about as financial manager in a branch office of a tobacco company in New York? Or as a copywriter in an ad agency with the tobacco company's account? Or as a cashier in a corner store dependent on tobacco sales?

How many degrees of separation are enough to feel we are not culpable?

Various forms of the "how close is too close" question come up in our role as consumers. Is it ethical to buy cosmetics from companies engaged in animal testing? To buy gasoline from companies with environmental law violations? To hold stock of a company in our retirement plan, the gains on which depend on robust sales of products we think unethical? To benefit from medical research performed in ethically questionable (or even repugnant) ways?

A related question: will we work for an organization whose ethical standards fall short of ours? Say we are asked to create sales incentives that encourage others to act unethically. What do we do? Finding ourselves in such a workplace puts us in a bind if we feel we are aiding an organization whose standards of behavior we don't agree with. So before we find ourselves in an ill-fitting enterprise, we face a decision: what company will we keep?

Say we are a prosecutor considering a job in an attorney general's office of a state with the death penalty. If we consider the death penalty unethical, do we consider it ethical to work in a system that backs it—even if we're not connected to the act?

One of our engineering students, a Hindu who considers all killing unethical, addressed proximity to the military in his code. First, he decided the use of his research by the military was ethical (if such happens). He reasoned that he was not responsible for how others use his work, which concerns how to make any organization more efficient. Second, he decided not to accept pay, even indirectly, from the military. When he came to understand he was hired for a project at Stanford through a grant from the military to his professor, he terminated his work at the end of an initial commitment.

In another case, an energy-efficiency consultant, who drafted a code with a consequentialist foundation, evaluated the ethics of investing in Philip Morris, a tobacco company. Although acknowledging the harm of tobacco, he concluded, "Ultimately, owning my tiny fraction of the company does not incur a net moral cost that outweighs the potential benefit to me, and so I view my investment as ethical. Most of the alternative investment options available included broad mutual funds that would have resulted in my ownership of a small stake anyway. This adds to my view that owning small stock positions is far enough away as to be ethically permissible."

DRAW SHARPER LINES. When we word positive ethics, we need to draw the line clearly. In contrast to negative ethics, positive ethics require us to state how far we will go. Suppose we want to adopt the proverbial "I will feed the hungry." Like Mother Teresa, we have given ourselves a full-time, global job—with unlimited overtime. Over 850 million people in the world are undernourished.[2]

Or what if we propose to stop harm? How far will we stick our necks out? Thousands of children, not to mention adults, die every year in armed conflicts.[3] Positive ethics pose another dilemma: how much do we reduce our own comfort to increase that of others? Unless we are thinking of becoming a saint, we will have to circumscribe our commitment.

Many people accept fuzziness when they draw their lines. This leaves them unsure of compliance with their standards. So when we refine our codes, the rule is, the more specific our positive injunctions, the better. One code reads, "I will oblige myself to donate at least 5 percent and no more than 10 percent of my disposable income toward charitable purposes."

One way to draw the line for some ethics is to define our ethical space as our immediate surroundings. If we are walking down the street and we hear or see someone in need, we will help. We will be a Good Samaritan. Although our code wouldn't prevent us from helping others, if we draw the line at immediate surroundings, we consider the extra step an act of virtue, not ethics.

CONSIDER A HIERARCHY. Another refinement that some people like to include in their code is an ethical hierarchy. If one ethic conflicts with another, which takes precedence? When will we accept one evil to avoid another? As the story of Kurt Gerstein showed, ethical hierarchies can be dangerous because they confuse the ethical issues and may lead us to do things we would later regret. At their root, they are just another way of choosing lesser evils.

At first pass, we might choose the most obvious hierarchy, placing avoiding harm in priority to avoiding theft, and in turn avoiding theft in priority to avoiding lies. This would have worked for the Hindu holy man in chapter 3. But if we test other scenarios, we realize a rigid hierarchy yields suspect results, owing to the divergent consequences of ethical compromise.

Ethical dilemmas occur only rarely, but adopting hierarchies to address them nonetheless remains problematic, because making trade-offs with the knowledge of certain ethical outcomes is impossible. Suppose we steal a car to take a sick friend to the emergency room. We believe we have placed avoiding harm above avoiding theft. But what if someone else had the car waiting for another life-or-death purpose? We incur responsibility for the consequences of our action, and in this case our action could cause death.

One variety of hierarchy dictates the priority of particular people. One code reads, "I believe in a consequentialist view of dealing with ethical situations I face. That being said, however, there are certain limitations I will impose on my possible actions. I shall use the utilitarianism viewpoint for major decisions that have to be made and will consider this utility according to the following hierarchy of recipients: (1) my family, (2) myself, (3) my friends, and (4) others."

This code states a common sentiment: if push comes to shove, I take care of my own first. Although the code provides clear guidance, it could allow reprehensible behavior. The extreme example: death-camp inmates conspire with guards to save themselves by aiding in the killing of others. Using hierarchies always poses the risk of engaging in unskillful ethical decision making, and for that reason we do not recommend them, even though many people prefer to include them in their code. We can often find clearer and more useful ways to think about ethical conflicts.

Failure Factors

By following the process in this chapter for drafting, testing, and refining our codes, we should not expect to come up with a perfect code. As we age, we will rethink our principles. We will probably never come up with a code "suitable for framing." Every word, phrase, principle, and rule is the result of judgment, and our judgment is sure to evolve and change.

Nonetheless, even our first draft of a code should be a practical tool to sharpen our thinking and change our behavior. We don't want to go to a lot of effort and not come up with concrete results. For some added advice on avoiding failure, here are six pitfalls:

CONFUSING PRUDENTIAL AND ETHICAL ISSUES. We fail to rid our code of prudential issues, and so bury the ethical ones.

At the risk of overemphasis: we need to avoid including prudential, nonethical issues in our code. The purpose of the code is to decide where to draw the line between right and wrong. Prudential commentary can overrun our code like vines overrun a jungle.

USING LOADED LANGUAGE. We fail to express ourselves in value-neutral language.

Euphemisms and cacophemisms prevent decision-making clarity. If we address abortion, we may use the default terms *pro-life* or *pro-choice*. But this loaded language veils the ethical issue. Who, after all, is against life or choice? The terms provide no basis for decision-making clarity. The ethical issue lies elsewhere.

We can recast our language to highlight what, for each of us, is the real issue. One code reads, "I will never kill an unborn fetus, nor ask someone to kill one, nor fund such a killing willingly . . . I will, however, provide emotional support to a friend who chooses to have an abortion, as long as I think that friend has put sufficient thought into her decision."

Another example of loaded language is the term *social justice*. It would be hard to find someone against justice, social or otherwise. So here again we need to ask, What is the real issue? Perhaps it is transferring money from the rich to the poor. If so, we need to make this plain. Yet another phrase is *cruelty to animals*. Is anyone in favor of cruelty? Perhaps the ethical issue is more accurately whether it is right or wrong to inflict pain on laboratory animals.

JUDGING THE ACTIONS OF OTHERS. We forget that our code is to help improve our own behavior, not judge that of others.

Be wary of statements that judge the actions of others. Although such judgments have their place, the place is not in an ethical code. Statements that reveal confusion include, "I support capital punishment." Or "I condone embryonic stem cell research." A code should express the behavior we condone in ourselves, not in others, and certainly not behaviors that are merely opinions of public policy.

If, say, we support capital punishment, the better question is, Would I personally take the life of another person when that person is guilty of a capital crime? Or would I personally remove embryos for stem cell research? Or use force to prevent its being done? Words like *condemn*, *support*, and *condone* are telltales of judging others. We need to redirect our attention from our views of society's implicit codes to our own personal code. A code is valuable for personal growth, not pointing fingers.

BASING ETHICS ON THE JUDGMENTS OF OTHERS. We mimic the inner voice of others instead of listening to our own.

We may simply adopt the ethics of our teachers, spiritual leaders, parents, friends, or leaders. We may be inclined to say, "I will not do anything my parents or friends will be ashamed of." Or "I will not do anything to dishonor my parents." But we need to come to our own conclusions. If our code does not stem from introspection, we won't embrace it, and it will fail to serve us.

Another issue that arises is the uncertainty regarding what other people think. A standard based on others' thoughts can be arbitrary and variable. What our friends are ashamed of today may be different from what they are ashamed of tomorrow. We should avoid a code that requires assessing someone else's emotional states to determine our own ethics.

MAKING PRAISEWORTHY BUT NOT LIVABLE STATEMENTS. We write a statement of aspirations we cannot possibly meet.

Avoid letting your code get too high-toned and ambitious. It should describe a more ethical version of you, raising the bar high but not out of reach. It should not describe "the perfect me." Beware if your code reads along these lines: "As a Christian (or Jew, Muslim, or Hindu), I believe in the Bible's (or Torah's, Qur'an's, or Mahabharata's) authority. When faced with ethical dilemmas, I will follow its ethical rules." Such a statement is a sign of too little reflection.

WRITING VAGUE STANDARDS. We make the same error our teachers always seemed to tag us for: we are vague or noncommittal.

The English teacher's perennial pet peeve: vagueness. Codes need to contain guidance for concrete actions we can draw in black and white. The issues in table 4-1 come up so often in life that only a vague code could evade them. Real commitments are more useful.

Ethical Owner's Manual

With an ethical code in hand, we prime ourselves for dealing with difficult and daily challenges. Without a code, we find it too easy to overlook, sweep aside, put behind us, and "let go" of ethical mistakes. With a code, we have a tool to act more quickly and without remorse. Our code helps us remain true to ourselves as we face life's predictable challenges. And it helps us remain true to other people, whose relationships we depend on.

If our mother is dying of cancer and she wants to know how long she has to live, do we tell her the truth? Presumably we will all face (or have faced) this question. What should (did) we decide? The introspection we engaged in to produce our code prepares us for such questions.

To cover so many contingencies, we may be tempted to create a long code. After all, the multiple avenues of thought taken during our reflections seem to push us in the direction of a complex road map. That's probably why many of our students produce long and complex codes. But the breadth of introspection need not result in thousands of words to cover hundreds of situations. The clearer our ethical thinking, the shorter our codes can be. The best codes are a set of principles with just a few exceptions, often chosen from table 4-1.

As the saying goes, "I only wrote this long, because I didn't have the time to make it shorter."[4] In other words, less is more. The same is true of codes, which should be immediately useful when we are tempted to do the wrong thing. If a code is long and has many exceptions, we probably haven't thought through the issues as well as we should have. Moreover, our code will then be hard to remember, and it will not be as helpful.

If we are to ask, "How do I know I have a good code?" the answer is, "When it describes the very best version of you that you can be." The "best" reflects a new, thoughtful ethical self: Skilled in drawing ethical distinctions. Cognizant of ethical trade-offs. Confident of ethical choices. Imbued with a sense of integrity—not a weakness for sacrificing honorable behavior on the altar of self-interest.

Yet a code has its limits. Preparing one is a bit like preparing to drive a new car by reading the owner's manual. We study standard emergency procedure in advance because things happen when we're not expecting them to. The time to read the manual (and commit principles to memory) is in an armchair, unchallenged by crisis.

When we are in a crisis, the code may not be enough. We need the faculty to make fresh decisions based on our code's principles. We need to know how to clarify the ethical issue, create alternatives, and choose not just the right action but the "best" action to build character and strengthen relationships. As we learn in the next chapter, we don't have to simply "go with our gut" to make skillful and creative decisions. We can arrive at a decision in a systematic fashion.

➤ Your Turn: Prototype Your Code

If you haven't already, now is the time to commit to an ethical code. Refine your core ethical principles, derived from chapter 3, using further reflection from this chapter. Note key exceptions to your principles, using table 4-1 as a guide. Remember that the most successful codes amount to a handful of principles plus some exceptions.

Now turn to appendix B, where we reprint several codes written by our students. Each balances principles with rules, fleshed out with personal opinions and examples. As you read the codes, mark them up to show where they clearly follow or diverge from our advice. Turn back to your own code. Refine it to simplify and strengthen it.

CHAPTER 5

Choose Action

Systematic Ethical Decision Making

*I cannot for want of sufficient premises, advise you what
to determine, but if you please I will tell you how.*

—Benjamin Franklin[1]

O N MARCH 13, 2006, six men were infused with a brand-new drug, TGN1412, in a research facility outside London, England. Within minutes, one of the men complained of a headache. Within hours, all six were rushed to Northwick Park Hospital with multiple-organ shutdown. Only massive doses of steroids, administered intravenously, along with mechanical ventilation and other high-tech support, brought the men back from the brink of death.[2]

The episode marked one of the most disastrous clinical drug trials—and triggered a storm of criticism. Why, observers asked, had researchers put healthy men at such risk?[3]

British authorities cleared researchers of wrongdoing.[4] The trial had been vetted and approved by regulators in both the United Kingdom and Germany, the home of TeGenero, the developer of the drug. Still, the debacle caused a global stir, enough so that the case of TGN1412 may well take its place as a classic in the annals of human research ethics.

TGN1412 was a novel drug aimed at fighting cancer and arthritis by stimulating immune cells in a new way. It was undergoing tests for the first time in humans. It posed a small risk of unprecedented side effects—in particular, a devastating inflammatory syndrome called a *cytokine storm*, in which the immune system attacks the body's own organs.[5] The test was conducted on healthy men whose main inducement for partici-pating was a £2,000 stipend.

The test bristled with ethical questions. One of the simplest: did re-searchers, who were testing a novel drug, disclose specific risks to test volunteers? Did the researchers omit information that would have sug-gested the chance of catastrophic side effects already witnessed in anal-ogous compounds? Or did they just use standard, business-as-usual consent language?[6]

We can never know the full inside story of the TGN1412 trial—in spite of reams of documents now open to the public. But we do know that it reaffirms an enduring lesson about ethical decision making: in challenging situations loaded with ethical issues—not to mention less dramatic, everyday cases—we can make smarter decisions by stopping long enough to follow a simple decision-making process:

1. **Clarify the ethical issue.** What is the basic ethical temptation we face?

2. **Create alternatives.** What acceptable, appealing, and even transformative options do we have?

3. **Evaluate the alternatives.** Which alternatives offer defensible, ethical responses?[7]

In the case of TGN1412, how could researchers have improved their decision making? Let's start by assuming they had stellar ethical princi-ples. Did they spend time clarifying potential ethical sensitivities in this situation? Did they consider alternatives that more fully took into account the point of view of healthy male test volunteers? Did they provide enough information to volunteers for them to be totally informed?

We all find ourselves at times facing challenging ethical temptations, whether under pressure to speed an inadequately tested product to market or to curry favor with someone by deceit. At such times, our code can often guide us to the right answer. But it may not guide us to the best answer. We can always make higher-quality decisions if we use a decision-making process to supplement our code, whether we are action- or consequence-based thinkers.

Quality Decisions

The first hurdle in making high-quality ethical decisions is simply over-coming the tendency not to think, which we discussed in chapter 1. Most of the time, we remain numb to critical issues, ignorant of our biases, and guided in decisions by age-old ruts. Remarkably, we compromise not just in situations as critical as the case of TGN1412. We do so in everyday life.

By referring to quality decisions, we mean decisions where we have followed a high-quality process and adhered to proven principles. This is not to be confused with high-quality outcomes, the results of the decision. None of us can know the future, which means we can make a good deci-sion and end up with a bad outcome; or we can make a bad decision and end up with a good outcome. Of course, in most cases, the worse the deci-sion, the worse the outcome.

In the case of TGN1412, clinical-trial designers decided to dose all six volunteers at once. It would have been a simple matter to wait a few hours or days between infusing each subject, to gauge initial side effects. The delay could have avoided untold harm. Was the researchers' decision bad—even though it adhered to established protocols? Or was it just the clinical trial's outcome that was bad? Some observers argued that lousy decisions were responsible for the debacle.[8]

On a much lighter subject, one of our favorite stories about failed eth-ical decision making is about a friend who, as a young man, was visiting his fiancée's parents for the first time. His future mother-in-law served him rhubarb pie, her prize dish. He hated rhubarb. Attempting to make a good impression, however, he said he loved rhubarb. It was his favorite. He choked down the pie with a smile.

Of course, given the delicate situation, it seemed a minor inconven-ience to feign liking the detested rhubarb. But now, thirty years later, he has racked up scores of episodes of lying about rhubarb to his mother-in-law, and swallowing the unpleasant stuff every time. He has carried on this deceit for decades—even while she goes to special pains to bake the pie for him every time he visits. The hole he has dug for himself gets deeper every year.

A petty situation, of course. How could he have known an innocent fib told at one meal, one day, during one episode of socializing, could send ripples of a ridiculous fraud across years of his life? But note how the story makes the same point as the TGN1412 case, only projected into a situation from everyday life: we often fail to be sensitive to ethical decision-making issues placed right before our eyes. We keep our heads down and plunge ahead, failing to take the steps necessary to make a quality decision.

Armed with the concepts and tools we've accumulated since chapter 1, we can better identify impending compromises and confidently put on the brakes. In the language of decision making, we can make time to respond instead of react. When we react, we act on reflex. Our actions reflect ignorance. When we respond, we act on reasoning. Our actions reveal thought.

Even if we have to make decisions on the fly, we can respond wisely. Without time to think, we can rely on our code, which represents forethought. Or we can tap on the brakes just long enough to guide our behavior in a better direction with a decision-making process. Even if we only have a few seconds or minutes, we still can use an abbreviated form of the process for decisions.

To be sure, all of this takes work. It does not come naturally to most of us. We will need to spend time to make it a habit. This will be especially hard if we have to change or reverse old habits. And yet that is what is required for ethical action based on responding rather than reacting.

In the past, we may have thought of ethical challenges as problems. But they also offer a chance to respond in ways in which we go one or several steps beyond minimally ethical actions. If we declare an opportunity for a quality decision, we create an opening to find the optimal way to build character and deepen relationships. We align ourselves with our values and meantime develop an ever deeper sense of integrity.

Step 1: Clarifying

The first and foremost step we must take is accurately describing the temptations we face. Depending on how we phrase the question, we highlight some concerns and shade others. If we highlight the right ones, the pivotal element of the decision reveals itself. We spotlight the issue. If we shade the wrong ones, the pivotal element remains in the dark—and so does our thinking. When we don't construct the right frame for our question, we go wrong from the start. It's that simple.

For simplicity, take the rhubarb case. How did our friend frame the challenge he faced? Did he recognize it as an ethical opportunity? A number of questions may have jumped to his mind: How do I get out of this jam? How do I make a good first impression on my future mother-in-law? How do I begin to build a solid, long-term relationship with my mother-in-law? Each question highlights a different concern. Which would have been the right one?

Because the wording of a question limits the description of the problem—and, knowingly or not, we all frame questions to make them manageable—our biggest mistakes in ethical decision making are mistakes in framing. Before we get past even the first step in decision making, we can erroneously limit our thinking.

Most of us fail to consciously frame our decisions. In the language of psychiatrists, we focus on the *presenting problem*. Patients often come to psychiatrists with a specific symptom. They can't sleep, for example. For therapists, the challenge is to go beyond the sleep problem to the underlying one. The same goes for our handling of the question in ethical decision making.

By practicing three techniques, we can more clearly see the question facing us:

- Describe the situation in value-neutral language.

- Separate prudential, legal, and ethical concerns.

- Frame questions in terms of relationships with other people.

Let's take an example. A mother is worried about her teenage son's forays on the Internet late at night.[9] She frets about the people he meets online, what they talk about, and what they may plan offline. More than anything, she wants to read his e-mail and track his surfing history. She doesn't want to confront him, because she is reluctant to cast doubt on his judgment. But she wants to know all is well.

After some rumination, she decides she is balancing two ethical issues: her son's right to privacy and her duty to protect her child from harm. Which concern gets priority? Given her frame for the question, she tentatively decides to read his e-mail in secret. Many of us would do the same: we would decide that a duty to prevent harm naturally trumps a right to privacy.

But let's apply the first of our three techniques for clarifying an ethical question—recasting the question in value-neutral language. We see that the mother has unwittingly framed her question with two value-laden phrases: *right to privacy* and *duty to prevent harm*. Both introduce bias.

Right and *duty* are common loaded words. They sound legitimate but have an obfuscating element. After all, in a free society, who could possibly be against a right to privacy? Or a duty to protect children? The phrasing is not useful as a means to separate right action from wrong.

By using value-neutral language, the mother can more clearly illuminate the specific ethical compromise she is tempted to make. If she uses simpler language, she is simply tempted to read her son's e-mail without permission. The high-minded issues of *rights* and *duties*—whether questions of ethics or not—cloud the more basic and naked question: should I deceive?

If neutral language alone doesn't reveal the true nature of an ethical question, we can try a second technique: disentangling prudential, legal, and ethical concerns. What are the legal concerns in this example? There are none. What are the ethical ones? The mother could again cite right to privacy and duty to protect children from harm.

At first, the privacy and harm concerns sound like pure, unadulterated ethical issues. But are they? One good way to attack this question—and most ethical questions—is to start with first principles. Does any aspect of the proposed action touch on the basic building blocks of ethics—namely, deceiving, stealing, or harming? If we have an ethical code, these issues cover familiar territory, and we know where we stand.

This is a critical point: when we are faced with framing an ethical question, we benefit greatly from first checking bare-bones ethical principles. (See table 4-1 in chapter 4.) Like most people, if the mother had embraced the sketchiest outlines of a code, she would probably have a principle about avoiding deception. What if she recast her question to highlight this more bare-bones issue? What if, again, she simply asked, Should I deceive my son?

Because life is complex, we often create complex ethical frames. We clothe workaday questions in fancy garb, covering basic ethical issues with stylish prudential accoutrements. We gravitate to the lofty and ponderous, creating "dilemmas by design." Right to privacy and duty to protect, because of their weightiness and their positioning at odds with each other, prevent us from framing the question more clearly.

In the case of the dutiful mother, she may realize she doesn't face mainly an ethical problem at all. She faces a parenting one. She doesn't need to spend hours debating ethical issues. She just needs to sit down and have a heart-to-heart talk with her child.

If the first two techniques don't clarify the ethical question, we can try a third. Ask, What impact will my actions have on this relationship? Our ethical actions are not just one-off transactions; they are a part of ongoing interactions with other human beings. By explicitly considering each relevant relationship, we bring long-term effects into sharper relief.

In the case of the mother, she could simply ask, Does covertly reading e-mail enhance the relationship with my son? Would it enhance relations with anyone? Does it add to the trust and goodwill that typify strong bonds between humans? Does it reinforce the faith one person has with another who shares a close connection?

Using value-neutral language. Clarifying prudential, legal, and ethical issues. Expressing issues in terms of relationships. Each of these three techniques reframes the ethical question, shifting our point of view, allowing us to see through the distorting influences of a situation. If the mother had used these three techniques, she would have three times come up with the same answer on whether to read her son's e-mail without permission: no. (If she followed consequence-based ethics, the answer could be more complicated.)

It's hard to overestimate how much shifting the question can reshape our perspective. An old story makes this point. Two monks who were heavy smokers would often smoke and pray together in the evening. They became concerned that their smoking habit was a sin. So they each asked their superior for guidance.

They met again the next day. The first was puffing away when the second arrived. "But the head of the monastery told me it was a sin," protested the second. "What did you ask him?" said the first. "I asked him if it was all right to smoke during our evening prayer, and he said no."

"Well," said the first monk, "I asked if it was all right to pray during our evening smoke, and he said it was just fine."

The story reminds us that reframed questions can overturn our thinking so easily that if we are in any doubt about whether we have appropriately posed the ethical question, we should try again. The rule is always, go slow in clarifying the right frame to go fast in making the right decision. Of course, if we have to make the decision quickly, we won't have the luxury of sleeping on our question. But with training, we will get increasingly adept, able to adjust the frame in moments.

Step 2: Creating Alternatives

Once we have established our ethical question, we come to generating alternatives for action. This is where the creativity in ethical living begins. We should aim to come up with multiple alternatives, at least three or four. Sometimes a creative alternative completely eliminates the ethical sensitivity. Other times, a creative alternative can turn ethical challenges into opportunities to deepen relationships.

Most of us are inclined to "satisfice," in the words of Nobelist Herbert A. Simon. As soon as we come up with an alternative we think is good enough, we act on it, rather than searching for an alternative that would be even better. Satisficing is a reasonable strategy for low-stakes decisions—where to eat lunch or what book to buy. But when relationships and character are at stake, it often leaves much to be desired. We then need a better way to think.

To help us skillfully create a range of choices, we can try several strategies:

- **Refrain or comply.** Choose alternatives that comply with minimum ethical standards, which may simply mean doing nothing.

- **Elevate.** Consider alternatives an ethical role model would take, which would be actions we would admire.

- **Transform.** Ask, "How would I act toward a loved one?" This means acting as we would toward our child or a romantic partner.

For a simple illustration, imagine you are new to a job. You are hanging out with your new colleagues, and one of them regales the group with a racist joke, which you find repugnant. You want to fit in and make a good impression, so you are tempted to not say anything. Your ethical code forbids deception, however, and you believe keeping quiet might give people the impression you approve of racist humor. This situation is now open to ethical question. What do you do?

The alternatives that occur to you initially might be:

Laugh with the group, pretending to enjoy the joke.

Speak up, expressing your displeasure.

When such awkward situations come up, we often say to ourselves, "I have no choice." But we always have a choice. Our impulsive thought, "My hands are tied," stems from reacting. If we respond instead—if we do the work to make a habit of responding—we can often choose not only to resist compromise but to comply, elevate, or transform.

Let's take comply. Here are some other alternatives, which may not be great, but they show displeasure at the joke:

Do nothing (at least you are not laughing with the group).

Frown.

Leave the group.

Quit your job.

To give ourselves the best chance of generating creative alternatives, we must avoid early critiquing. Critical thought quickly shuts down creative thought. For example, while quitting may seem extreme in this circumstance, it may bring to mind more interesting alternatives.

Now what would an ethical role model do?

Talk to the joke teller in private later.

Talk to a human resources manager or your boss about the incident.

Lobby for tolerance training.

What about transformational alternatives? What would you do if you loved both the person telling the racist joke and the others in the group?

What if your best friend had made a racist joke; how would you want to respond? One effective transformational alternative is simply telling the whole truth. Telling the whole truth often has little initial appeal because figuring out what the truth is—our truth—is often hard. The whole truth in this situation is not, "I find racist jokes repugnant; please do not tell them in my presence."

The whole truth is often more like this: "I'm grateful to you for including me in this conversation, because I'm new at this company, and I really want to fit in and do a good job. And your joke bothered me. I was tempted not to say anything to better fit in, but then I don't want to start our relationship by pretending to be something I'm not. I'm sorry if this puts you in an awkward situation, but I could really use your help in figuring out how to respond in situations like this."

When we tell our whole truth, our words have authenticity, which has the power to deepen relationships. We may find our frankness leads to a break in relationships. But if others take offense at our truths, we have to question the value of our relations with these people in the first place. Most people respect truth spoken with grace, respect, and humility.

Consider another challenging ethical situation. This one comes from a nurse interviewed after visiting a patient. In the nurse's words: "I was in a nursing home [caring for a] woman who had Alzheimer's and she said: 'Oh, where is my husband?' and I had been told that this lady had been a widow for about 15 years, and I'd looked at this woman and said to her: 'Oh sweetie, your husband died 15 years ago,' and the woman's grief was instantaneous. It was like I was delivering the news for the first time about her husband's death, and I felt devastated . . . and I thought, 'Oh my god, now I have this mourning woman . . .' and in hindsight . . . if that ever happens to me again I might just say: 'He's out in the garden or he's gone away or he'll be back' only because I know that [she'll] forget about it in a couple of minutes."[10]

Let's suppose that the nurse had an ethical code with a rule to tell the whole truth. Her action was certainly ethical, but was it the only alternative? Her real range of alternatives might have looked like this:

Lie about the husband's death.

Do nothing (ignore the woman).

Say, "I don't know where your husband is."

Tell the plain truth (as the nurse did).

Leave the room.

Ask, "When did you see him last?"

Redirect the conversation to memories of her husband.

Since the nurse's ethical code forbids lying, the first two alternatives represent giving in to temptation. But as in the previous example, other alternatives exist. She has a range of ways to act ethically, if she responds rather than reacts, and her response need not take much time. She can elevate or transform the situation while genuinely addressing the patient's concern about her husband.

Telling the whole truth does not mean we answer every question asked of us. If someone asks us how much money we made last year, we can simply say, "I do not want to reveal that information." Alternatively, we could answer with a question: "Why do you want to know?" We can refuse to divulge information and still follow an ethic of telling the whole truth.

This process of coming up with alternatives can be applied to many of the cases already discussed in this book. Before Kurt Gerstein joined the Waffen SS in World War II, he tried many ways to overcome his core ethical challenge: how to avoid denying his Christian beliefs and violating Christian ethical principles. He joined protests, issued pamphlets, and gave speeches to young people.[11] His goal was to reform the party from within.

Gerstein was so outspoken that he was ousted from the party. He persisted with his protests, and although he considered himself a patriot, the Gestapo put him in a concentration camp in 1938. Over six and a half weeks, the camp nearly broke him. Of the party, he wrote, "Their cultural aim is to destroy not only the Catholic and Evangelical churches but every form of serious belief in God in Germany."[12]

In the end, Gerstein gave up on protests and managed to clear his name with the Nazi party. He then chose to anoint himself as a Nazi whistleblower, a man with an intimate view of the workings of Hitler's most reviled team of henchman. When he adopted this alternative, however, he still had a range of others to choose from:

Do nothing (the course most of his countrymen took).

Give more speeches (and risk repeated jailing).

Lead protests or a campaign of civil disobedience.

Challenge the government in court.

Initiate undercover espionage.

Set up an underground railroad to help people emigrate.

Emigrate.

Fight.

Commit suicide (his ultimate fate).

Self-immolate (public-protest suicide).

We cannot presume to put ourselves in Gerstein's shoes. He was a man committed to doing good, tortured by the twisted machinations of the Nazi regime. Yet he did have other alternatives, choices ranging from groveling and pleading to spitting in their faces.

Records from his life suggest he agonized over many scenarios. Could he have come up with an alternative that both complied with his ethical standards and helped him fight the Nazi menace? Could he have avoided the evil of choosing the lesser of two evils? What if Gerstein had acted toward his victims as toward a loved one?

We could draft a similar range of alternatives for the e-mail-reading mother, the rhubarb-hating son-in-law, the embattled clinical-trial designers, the employee stuck in a job with a questionable company—about so many people facing common ethical challenges. Rarely are ethical answers binary. Like ethical questions, they come in a range of colors.

We can easily see that the more interesting, attractive, and workable alternatives we have, the greater our capability to avoid or even transform temptation. We should remember not to judge our alternatives too much as we devise them—a cardinal rule of brainstorming. This is not a time to edit and audit. It's a time to open up, to let ideas run. Even if we only have minutes to make a decision, we can quickly assess a menu of options.

Step 3: Evaluating Alternatives

The last step in making a quality decision is to test the ethical quality of the alternatives, to judge, edit, and audit, to distinguish between good, bad, better, and best. Whether we are action- or consequence-based in our leanings, we can use four testing steps:

- Evaluate alternatives against our code. (What would our code have us do?)

- Evaluate against our ethical role model. (What would our role model do?)

- Test for reciprocity. (What would the other-shoe test suggest we do?)

- Test for universality. (What if everybody did it?)

When it comes to evaluating alternatives against our code, we will often face obvious choices. We have committed ourselves to behaving according to actions deemed right or wrong. We have erected standards and stand by them. Unless the alternatives fall in a gray area, our modus operandi is straightforward: our code defines our standards, so we let our code dictate our behavior.

After we strike choices that violate our code, we test the remaining options against what our role model would think. More generally, we can draw on any of the tests from chapter 2 that hold us to a higher standard. In addition to the role-model test, we can use the mother's test or the front-page test.

Next we test for reciprocity, again drawing on distinctions we learned in chapter 2. We test our alternatives with various metal rules—in particular, variations of the Golden Rule. Each metal rule addresses reciprocity of some kind, so we put ourselves in the shoes of another and assess the fit of our alternatives. Once again, we borrow from chapter 2 to use the other-shoe test, the biased-language test, or the loved-one test.

Some questions we could ask: If we are on the delivering end of an inappropriate joke at work, would we want someone else to frown, leave the room, or talk with us later? If we were a patient in an Alzheimer's ward, would we prefer that a nurse tell the truth, redirect the conversation, or do nothing? If we were a victim of genocide, would we prefer that Kurt Gerstein go undercover, emigrate, or carry on protests at the risk of getting jailed anew?

If we are unsure about the meaning of reciprocity, we can gain added perspective through a closer look at Immanuel Kant's thinking. Kant actually described three formulations of his "categorical imperative." The first, introduced in chapter 2, was that an action is ethical if it can be willed as universal law. The second is that an action is ethical if we treat a person as an end and not a means. The third is that it must be possible for an ethical behavior to be self-imposed by each person.

The most useful may be the second because it focuses on reciprocity in relationships. Kant wrote in 1785, "So act as to treat humanity, whether in thine own person or in that of another, in every case as an end withal, never as a means only."[13] This is a long way of saying, Don't use people. Kant is in essence saying, in ethically sensitive situations, treat everyone you meet as a full human being, deserving the same ethical consideration.

Outsiders following the debacle of the TGN1412 drug trial could wonder whether researchers tested their disclosure alternatives with reciprocal thinking. Had one of the subjects been a loved one, would the researchers have more explicitly explained that the drug altered the immune system? Would they have highlighted the risks of a cytokine storm, which earlier tests of analogous drugs had hinted could happen? Were they using their subjects "as a means only"? Were there alternatives they could have chosen to do a better job of telling the "whole truth"?

Tests for reciprocity would also have called into question the complexity of the TGN1412 consent form. It was over five thousand words long. Almost a third of the sentences were written at graduate-school level. Could the researchers have produced an alternative form? Could they have given subjects extra time to examine it and talk with their own loved ones about their decision? Observers suggest that researchers erred not only by understating risks but by rushing subjects through the decision.[14]

As we test for reciprocity, we can also test for universalizability. This test brings us back to the first formulation of Kant's categorical imperative. Take again the example of the mother tempted to read her son's e-mail. Suppose she created a list of alternatives as follows:

Disconnect the family's Internet connection.

Read e-mail in secret.

Do nothing.

Ask her son whether she can read the e-mail.

Ask her son to tell her about his e-mail.

Talk to her son about e-mail dangers.

Tell the whole truth.

Which of these responses would the mother want to universalize? That is, which ones would she want everyone (including her son) to follow all the time? It seems doubtful she would want to universalize the practice of secretly reading another's e-mail. Disconnecting the Internet connection and doing nothing don't seem universalizable either.

One alternative that gets too little attention is simply asking permission. If we were like the mother, we could simply ask our child's permission. If we are thinking about taking home supplies from the office stationery cabinet, we can ask the boss whether it's OK. If we are tempted to take home an attractive menu from a restaurant, we can simply ask the waiter whether it's OK. Although painfully obvious, just asking permission can sometimes resolve sticky ethical questions.

The most powerful alternative, here again, may be to tell the whole truth. The mother could sit down with her son and share her dilemma: "I fear for your safety, which tempts me to read your e-mail without your permission. But I greatly respect your privacy, and I want to set an example of trustworthy behavior you can follow. So I have a dilemma; what should we do?"

Once we have evaluated our alternatives, if we are action-based, we will often readily see the best choice. At the very least, we will be able to rule out alternatives in conflict with our ethical code. No research studies, public-opinion polls, or cost-benefit analyses will change our minds. Action-based decision makers do not balance ethical criteria with prudential consequences. The principles in the code represent the floor of behavior.

Accounting for Consequences

If we are consequentialists, making quality decisions becomes more difficult. In addition to ethical considerations, we must evaluate prudential and legal ones. We must choose which principles we are willing to compromise to achieve a greater good, and then specify trade-offs. This means that if we are drug-trial designers, we will have to ask, Do we put small groups of human subjects at higher risk to speed up our trial, while not telling the subjects, to more quickly reap gains for mankind? If we are undercover agents for a Nazi-like regime, do we tolerate complicity in a killing machine to pass on testimony that will prevent atrocities in the future?

To take the consequentialist approach, combining legal and prudential considerations with ethical, we must add three steps to our process:

- Characterize consequences of each alternative.

- Assess uncertainties.

- Evaluate trade-offs.

Like the other thinking we have done so far, these analytical steps can take minutes or hours, depending on the needs of the situation. Consider an example of a decision made by executives at Google in 2006. The question was whether and how to change the way the company did business in China, whose government demanded censorship as a condition of doing business, an anathema to the founding vision of Google.[15] This case shows that the company's leaders had several alternatives, each of which required that they characterize consequences, assess uncertainties, and evaluate trade-offs.

From a business point of view, Google in the early 2000s was in a jam: Chinese censors were blocking the flow of Chinese-language Google.com search results into China. The homegrown Chinese search engine Baidu was rapidly amassing market share. Baidu operated unfettered by the so-called Great Firewall of China, a censorship machine that bogged down Google data flow from the United States through the handful of fiber-optic lines entering China.

Google's business alternatives came from two ends of a spectrum. At one end was sticking with the status quo and putting up with delivering

Chinese citizens a slow, balky, and Chinese-censored search engine. At the other end was moving Google servers onto Chinese soil, self-censoring search results, and competing at high speeds with the local Baidu whiz kids (along with Yahoo! and Microsoft).

The second variety of alternatives posed a simple ethical question: should Google work with Chinese authorities in censoring and thus supplying incomplete search results? Owing to Chinese law and the sensibilities of China's leaders, Google would have to voluntarily strip out sites linked to such terms as *Falun Gong*, *Tibet*, and *Tianamen Square*. So the question, in essence, was, Should Google become a partner with a regime dedicated to systematically deceiving its citizenry?

For Google executives, the decision would depend (in part or whole) on the company's and the executives' ethical codes, which we don't know. However, the company did make a splash during its public stock offering by using the phrase "Don't be evil" as a guiding mantra. And from public records, it would appear that Google executives demonstrated a consequence-based decision-making approach.

Let's apply the three new decision-making steps to Google's situation. First, let's characterize the potential consequences of each alternative. (See figure 5-1.)

If Google moves its servers to China and self-censors, the top branch in figure 5-1, the company achieves incremental prudential benefits, PB. But

FIGURE 5-1

The Google China decision

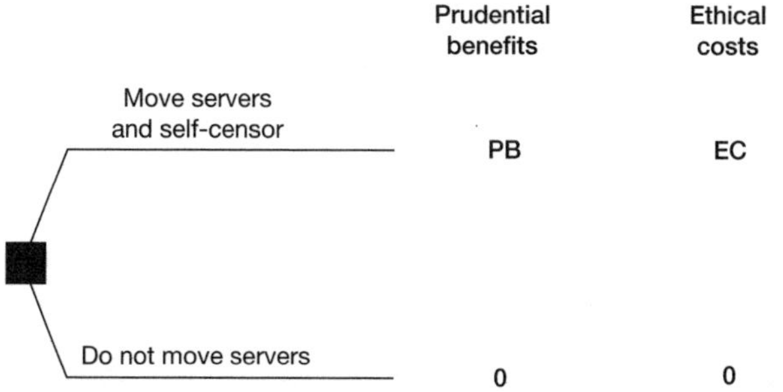

	Prudential benefits	Ethical costs
Move servers and self-censor	PB	EC
Do not move servers	0	0

these benefits come at an ethical cost, EC. For a consequentialist, ethical compromise is justified if the prudential benefits outweigh the ethical costs—if PB > EC. While this sounds simple, it can be challenging in practice for three reasons: long time horizons, time pressures, and uncertainty.

Long-term consequences are often not given enough attention. Simply picking an appropriate time horizon can be difficult. For Google, when was the right time to measure prudential benefits such as market-share gains? In three months? One year? Five years? And when was the right time to measure the ethical costs? After this decision was made? After the company sees whether any other compromises follow the first?

The negative consequences of ethical compromise sometimes take a while to emerge. Take our rhubarb-hating friend. If he had considered the thirty-year implication of his deception, he may not have pretended to like the pie. While Google may achieve short-term market-share improvements, it may incur unintended long-term costs from this compromise.

Time pressure amplifies the distortions in a consequence-based approach. As we saw with the thinking traps in chapter 1, when we are in the throes of an ethical situation, we may have a hard time figuring out our ethical principles. Likewise, we may find it difficult to figure out the price at which we are willing to compromise our principles. We also have prudential and legal issues competing for our attention. This makes it even more important for consequentialists to keep their code and its bedrock principles visible and distinct—even if they countermand them for the greater good.

Consequentialists also have to consider uncertainty. Few decisions are as simple as figure 5-1. They more often look like figure 5-2.

If Google moves its servers to China and self-censors, it has no guarantee it will achieve its hoped-for prudential benefits. A myriad of uncertainties outside its control may interfere: competitive responses from Baidu, more intervention from the Chinese government, effects on its reputation from poor public relations. With probability, p, Google will achieve the significant market-share improvement it hopes for, the top branch on "market-share uncertainty," and achieve benefits, PB. Then again, with probability, 1–p, it may not see any market-share improvement, represented by the bottom branch on "market-share uncertainty." Whether or not it sees market-share gains, it still incurs ethical costs, EC, by going down the self-censor path.

FIGURE 5-2

The Google China decision with uncertainty

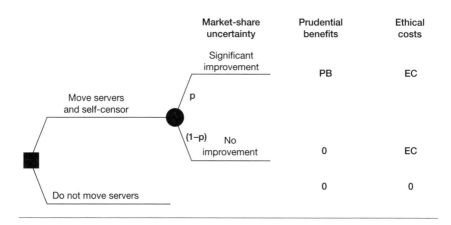

To put the entire picture together: Google must factor the chance (p) of significant improvement into the overall equation. Although a probabilistic analysis is beyond the scope of this book, we can make a number of observations.[16] First, balancing consequences can be hard and time-consuming work. While prudential decisions may require similar rigor, ethical considerations raise the stakes.

Second, we must be careful during consequence-based thinking not to give up on our ethical responsibilities. Some people think of consequentialism as "the ends justify the means." But when we face uncertainty, that saying is not exactly true. More accurate: "Our forecasted ends justify the means." Remember that ethics applies to our decisions, not to our outcomes. To say that we are ethical if the ends end up being good is to shift responsibility for our ethical behavior from ourselves to fate.

In the case of Google, executives could control whether or not they deployed servers in China. They could not control the responses of their competitors. In other words, ethical responsibility is attached to the beliefs for making the move, not to market-share outcomes. Our ethics are completely within our control, and regardless of what the future holds, we must take responsibility for our ethics at the time we make decisions.

Although we cannot know the details of Google's inside discussions, we do know that when all the facts were in, Google launched Google.cn in January 2006, a Chinese-language search engine based in Beijing with self-censored search results. The action outraged many in the United States, even though Google.cn search results came with a disclaimer that results were filtered. Lawmakers in Washington called for hearings. On February 15, 2006, in a session called "The Internet in China: A Tool for Freedom or Suppression?" Congressman Tom Lantos of California declared, "Instead of using their power and creativity to bring openness and free speech to China, they have caved in to Beijing's outrageous but predictable demands, simply for the sake of profit . . . They enthusiastically volunteered for the Chinese censorship brigade."[17]

Elliot Schrage, Google vice president of global communications and public affairs, defended the company's actions, saying, "Based on what we know today and what we see in China, we believe our decision to launch the Google.cn service in addition to our Google.com service is a reasonable one, better for Chinese users and better for Google."

Schrage's comments suggest Google weighed the prudential costs and benefits along with the ethical costs and benefits and went ahead. He elaborated in written testimony: "The requirements of doing business in China include self-censorship—something that runs counter to Google's most basic values and commitments as a company. Despite that, we made a decision to launch a new product for China—Google.cn—that respects the content restrictions imposed by Chinese laws and regulations . . . our decision was based on a judgment that Google.cn will make a meaningful—though imperfect—contribution to the overall expansion of access to information in China."[18]

Schrage added later, under fire by the Congressional committee, "This was not something we did enthusiastically or something that we're proud of at all." The Google case shows just how difficult the challenge can be for consequentialists. We can trade off all kinds of ethical principles for the benefit of prudential gains. In the end, Google left itself vulnerable to accusations it sacrificed ethical standards for the sake of gaining Asian market share. One sure prudential cost was blemishing its reputation as an honest broker of information. At least in China, users of Google will never know what results have been filtered out or even whether the filters change over time because of Chinese government demands or perhaps Google's business reasons.

Google also raises an age-old issue that might be a worthy item in an ethical code. Should we deal with rogue persons (or countries)? Should we engage them or isolate them? Should we play along with unethical players, hoping to coax or kindle reforms? Or should we shun them, hoping to motivate change? And most important, do their actions and behaviors change the way we think about right and wrong actions for ourselves?

If we embrace an action-based view, the answer is often easy. We follow our ethical code regardless of the situation or the other person involved. If that means we accept lower market share or profits, so be it. If we are consequentialists, the equation becomes more complicated. We face a weighty round of gathering information and trading off pluses and minuses. In particular, we must assess what other compromises we might have to face once we begin associating with an organization whose ethics are at odds with our own.

Skilled Ethical Thinking

The split between action- and consequence-based approaches becomes especially clear as we work through ethical decisions. Let's return to an earlier example to look at the risk of consequence-based thinking in another personal decision. Recall from chapter 1 Karl Schultze, the I. A. Topf and Sons engineer who designed and installed systems for cremation ovens for the Auschwitz concentration camp. Put yourself in the shoes of Schultze, who surely knew what the ovens were for. You have a family, a mortgage, and a future to protect.

Now suppose Schultze had, before the war, committed to an ethical code that said, "I will not kill except in self-defense." Suppose further that he had decided he would not work for a company that made equipment to kill innocent people. Both are reasonable presumptions, the kinds of decisions we would all easily make, especially in peacetime.

Now the war begins. If Schultze is action-based, what does he do when the orders to build systems for Auschwitz come in? What happens when he is asked to install them? He refuses to do the work. His decision is simple: he quits. In so doing, he demonstrates more ethical skill and willpower than the average German in World War II (and the average human across history).

Schultze suggested in his testimony, however, that he was not an action-based thinker. He was afraid his boss, Ludwig Topf, would fire him. He was worried about being arrested by the Nazis. So he followed orders.

In other words, he balanced ethical considerations with prudential ones. He weighed the benefits, costs, risks, and ethical implications. And he decided to stick with Topf.

In many ways, Schultze's story presents the danger that faces all of us. We can get trapped by our thinking into a string of consequence-based decisions we regret. Perhaps Schultze could have written a different story for himself—if he had sensitized himself to ethical compromise before the war. If he had learned about ethical distinctions. If he had a rigorous code. If he had applied ethical principles in a systematic way to make a *quality* decision on principle, not on circumstance. And if he had made all of these things a habit.

Schultze's story reminds us that our first challenge, to avoid compromise, is not to be taken lightly. Our next, to do the right thing, can be a signal achievement when we are under duress. The third, using ethical challenges as opportunities to make quality decisions, to elevate and even transform relationships, may seem out of reach altogether.

In the next two chapters, however, we will show how we can go well beyond the average. As we learn to become more skillful ethical thinkers, we can use our skills to come up with alternatives—and actions—that are much more gratifying than mere compliance. Whether we are action- or consequence-based, we can make a habit of transforming ethical challenges into opportunities to change relationships forever.

➤ Your Turn: Use Your Decision Tools

Recall the anecdote you summarized in chapter 1. Apply the tools from this chapter to come up with "good," "better," and "best" alternatives to your original action. Which alternative would you choose today in view of what you have since learned? Which alternative would have most strengthened your relationships?

CHAPTER 6

Transform Life

Skillful Decision Making
in Personal Life

Every conquering temptation represents a new fund of moral energy. Every trial endured and weathered in the right spirit makes a soul nobler and stronger than it was before.

—Attributed to William Butler Yeats

I N 1937, German businessman John Rabe faced a temptation many Nazis faced in World War II: to go along and be quiet at the sight or knowledge of genocide. Unlike men such as Karl Schultze, however, Rabe didn't go along. Rather than become an agent of lies, theft, and harm, he became an agent of truth and a protector of life. While many Germans succumbed to ethical desensitization and faulty thinking, Rabe remained faithful to higher ethical values.

On December 13, 1937, fifty thousand Japanese troops swept into the Chinese capital city of Nanking, on the vanguard of a major Japanese invasion of China. The city, an ancient center of government and culture, fell easily to Japanese forces. Damage from the initial assault was light.[1]

But in the ensuing days, Japanese troops went on a rampage, burning one-third of the city and terrorizing its people. Brutalities included rape, massacre, vivisection, and cannibalism. At least 260,000 civilians died at the hands of crazed soldiers unrestrained by their commanders.

Rabe was leader of the Nazi party in Nanking. He was the face of Germany, a staunch ally of Japan. He refused to aid the Japanese, and led other Western expatriates in creating the Nanking safety zone. In an island of urban buildings, he sheltered 250,000 Chinese. At great personal risk, he roamed the streets to stop pillage, murder, and sexual violation and mutilation, to the point of pulling a rapist off a young girl.

In *The Rape of Nanking*, the late author Iris Chang recounts the story of Rabe's work. Even before Japanese troops ran amok, he wired Hitler to request that the Japanese grant a safety zone. As atrocities spread, he protested repeatedly to Japanese diplomats. He telegraphed Hitler, who, by Rabe's account, interceded to redirect random bombing to military targets.

But Rabe's appeals made no real difference to civilians on the ground. The atrocities intensified.

When the carnage abated, Rabe returned to Germany, secreting a film of the barbarities with him. For his actions, Germany's secretary of state awarded him the Service Cross of the Red Cross Order. Rabe lectured about the massacre and showed his film in Berlin. He sent a report and the film to Hitler and his right-hand man, Hermann Goering. As promised to the people of Nanking, he publicized the heinous acts of Japanese soldiers.

Though few of us will experience the trials of Rabe, his story shows how individuals can transcend the darkest of ethical temptations. Rabe had every chance to compromise, to ignore and even abet the savagery. But he chose another alternative: to protect the civilians victimized by one of mankind's monstrous turns toward evil.

Our virtuous inclinations may not match those of Rabe. But we can take inspiration from him and seek to exercise the same skills to transcend temptation. Our journey started in chapter 1 with sensitizing ourselves to compromise. It continued with learning ethical distinctions (chapter 2), choosing ethical touchstones (chapter 3), and crafting an ethical code (chapter 4). It culminates in chapters 6 and 7 as we learn to use the decision-making process from chapter 5 to transform ethical challenges into revitalized relationships and character.

Choosing to Avoid

An ounce of prevention is worth a pound of cure. The best way to deal with many unethical or ethically debatable situations is to avoid them. Avoidance is much easier than blundering into an awkward situation. So always try avoiding before transforming. In the same way we use our ethical code to prepare for ethical challenges, we use our heightened sensitivity to anticipate and avoid dilemmas on the horizon.

One of the most useful decisions we can make is to refuse to join causes, groups, and organizations whose ethics are inconsistent with our own. Once we are inside a group, we can't easily walk out on our obligations. When an ethical temptation gets pushed in our direction, we may face a choice between violating our ethics and violating the norms of the organization. Too often we encounter bad organizational fits. Feeling trapped, we may fashion rationalizations that lead us to break our ethical code. But we can minimize this predicament, if, before we join organizations, we check them for alignment with our ethics.

We once heard a story about youth baseball. At the end of the regular season, a group of small towns each fielded two teams to compete in playoffs. The better boys were named to each town's A team, and the rest the B team. In short order, the A team in one particular town lost and was knocked out of contention. The B team advanced to the semifinals. When the B team's coach posted his starting lineup, the team's players (and parents) were surprised: the coach had drafted a pitcher from the A team as the starter.

To many parents of the B team, the draft amounted to rigging the game. One of the parents protested to the coach at the sidelines. The coach replied that he made the substitution for the boys' benefit. After all, he said, none of the boys enjoyed getting into a game and not doing well. The coach, though talented and well liked, did not feel the substitution was unethical. The parents felt it was cheating. There was clearly a mismatch between ethical codes.

Whether the organization is a sports team, a community group, or a youth organization, clashes between personal and organizational ethics happen all the time. For that reason, it's best to be careful which groups we join. If we see that a coach justifies what we consider ethical compromises for the sake of winning, or for the sake of everyone having a good time, we can choose to simply avoid the association.

When ethical questions do arise, it often feels too late. We may get swept along by events. In the baseball game, many parents felt they were unwitting accomplices in deceiving the other team—played out with their children taking it all in. Somewhat to the parents' relief, their children's team lost, which at least eliminated the ethical bind of winning a play-off seat improperly.

As our skill in applying ethical decision-making principles improves, we will encounter fewer situations of this kind. Instead, we can shift our focus more to the opportunities to use ethical action to transform ourselves and relationships with others. To create such opportunities, we focus on three skills:

- Finding the whole truth. Clarifying our motivations and fears, finding truths enabling us to act authentically.

- Framing issues as relationships. Creating alternatives by considering how our actions will affect other people, both now and over the long term.

- Raising the reciprocity bar. Asking, as we test our alternatives, not just how we would like to be treated but how we would like our loved ones to be treated.

In the end, we recognize more fully that ethics gives us not only the clarity to take the right action but the wisdom to create opportunities to do right by other people. As we keep the focus not on transactions but on those around us, we find that gains with people are enduring; gains during transactions, fleeting. Our job is to summon the will and imagination to focus on the enduring.

Transform Lies: Tell the Whole Truth

When we do find ourselves faced with the temptation to compromise, most commonly we are tempted to lie. Partly because lies are so common, especially white lies, we often consider them harmless, necessary, and reasonable. To reiterate, however, telling lies creates barriers in relationships. Instead, we can convert temptations to tell lies, little or big, into opportunities to transform relationships.

Consider how our rhubarb-hating friend could have turned around his white lie—if he had taken the time to grasp the whole truth of the moment. And if he had thought about the full effect on the mother of his fiancée. And if he had guided himself with the Golden, or platinum, or diamond rules.

Telling lies to mothers-in-law, of course, is a long-standing tradition for some people. But the basic principles of transformation work just as well for mothers-in-law as for anyone else. It starts with finding the whole truth.

The "whole truth" is harder to determine than we might think. In the rhubarb story, the truth lay buried. Maybe it was something like this: "Thank you for thinking of me when you made this rhubarb pie. I appreciate your effort and generous welcome. This is difficult for me to say because I love your daughter and I want our relationship to start off well. But I have to admit that I have never liked rhubarb."

Our friend would have had to realize why he was initially tempted to deceive—namely, that he wanted to make a good impression and thought the new relationship could not tolerate the truth. He would have had to dig inside himself to unearth these feelings. But the effort could have had an appealing reward. The whole truth has power because, by admitting our vulnerabilities and showing the courage to reveal them, we can deepen our most meaningful relationships.

Telling the truth in this fashion requires that we focus on people, not transactions. Instead of worrying about issues like the results of an event—embarrassment and awkwardness—we concern ourselves with the results of our relationship with a person. A good way to do this is to keep in mind the test of reciprocity. If we were making pie for a potential new relation, would we want to be lied to? More likely we would want to get to know the person better.

Doing the work to tell the whole truth means that we care enough about others to put the effort in, to face up to our fears, and to take an emotional risk. In the rhubarb story, since our friend didn't opt for the truth, he created a persistent, lifelong separation between himself and his mother-in-law. Creating this kind of separation might strike some children-in-law as not such a bad idea, but we wouldn't want to create it through unskilled or ignorant thinking.

Meeting in-laws (or parents) is a classic setup for testing the strength of our ethical skillfulness. The meeting means a lot to our partner. It is often stressful, uncertain, and awkward, because we hunger to make a good impression, and we worry that a mishap could distress our partner or rattle our relationship. Feeling the pressure, we can slide into mistruths. Perhaps if more people were skilled at telling the whole truth in emotionally charged situations, more mother-in-law relationships would be meaningful.

The notion of using the whole truth to transform relationships has a storied place in myth. American children learn how six-year-old George Washington, the first president, chopped down a cherry tree outside his father's house. The story, long believed, is a legend, created by biographer Mason Locke Weems. Like some authors today, Weems understood in 1809, when he wrote *The Life of Washington*, that letting facts get in the way of the story was no way to sell books.

And yet Weems, a liar himself, apparently also understood how to create a powerful ethical parable. Not only did George admit to felling the tree with his new hatchet. His father responded to the truth with joy: "Run to my arms, you dearest boy, run to my arms; glad am I, George, that you killed my tree; for you have paid me for it a thousand fold. Such an act of heroism in my son, [has] more worth than a thousand trees, though blossomed with silver, and their fruits of purest gold."[2]

We embrace stories in which truth transforms relationships. We see them in movies and the media, when characters reach points of insight and then go on to use the deeper truths to spur reconciliation with friends or loved ones. We can take advantage of this transformational power more often in real life.

Recall the story about the author lying to the agricultural inspector about tomatoes at California's border. What a perfect time this would have been for the author to cultivate his relationship with his children. But he didn't recognize the opportunity, and squandered it, although he then capitalized on his transgression to conduct many fruitful conversations thereafter.

Or think of the celebrity stories from earlier in the book. Consider historian Stephen Ambrose, whose plagiarism sullied an extraordinary career. He could have turned the temptation to take shortcuts into a sterling reputation—as opposed to burdening his children with defending his honor after his death. Or recall pitcher Kenny Rogers, who almost certainly lied about pine tar on his hand. He pitched a great game even after he removed it, but he could never restore his relationship with baseball fans.

And then there was U.S. President James K. Polk, who lied his way into starting a war with Mexico. He had many ways to truthfully secure a better relationship with lawmakers and the American public (let alone with Mexico). But he dealt a blow to his legacy by his untruths. And his duplicitous precedent has, arguably, damaged relations between presidents and citizens ever since.

Using the truth to deepen relationships is not a new idea. But we can rededicate ourselves to it. When we are tempted to tell half-truths, give false impressions, fake personal achievements, or be false in any number of ways, we can stop ourselves and ask, What is the whole truth? Who are we affecting? How can we do unto them as they would like us to? This is not a matter of just doing right, or good, but of nurturing relationships in the community in which we live.

Kant said, "By a lie a human being throws away and, as it were, annihilates his dignity as a human being."[3] But the corollary to Kant's warning is an insight we can benefit from: By the whole truth, we restore dignity and use it to revitalize our lives.

Transform Deception

Another productive source of opportunities to transform relationships is the temptation to deceive. Like lying, deception is ubiquitous, and we are similarly quick to fall for an immediate transactional gain at the expense of a relationship loss. Even worse, we may congratulate ourselves on our ability to deceive without "technically" telling a lie. But there is no ethical difference. In clever deception, we only compound the problem by fooling ourselves as well. As if we needed proof, studies show that people in romantic relationships experience the most positive relations when they do not engage in deception, and believe their partners refrain as well.[4]

To explore why this is so, recall the vignette from chapter 1 in which a student declines a friend's invitation to a movie because he wants to chill out in front of the television. He suggests the reason is that he has a lot of homework—which is true, but beside the point. Imagine if the student had instead paused a moment to find the truth and tap into it to deepen his relationship with a good friend.

The whole truth might have sounded something like this: "Thank you for asking me to the movies. I would really rather watch TV tonight, but I am afraid that when I say this, you may think I don't value your company. I do. I would be happy to go another time. But tonight, I just want to watch TV. Let me know tomorrow how the movie was."

The circumstances of this story may seem trivial, but that helps illustrate a crucial point. Before telling the whole truth, we have to realize why we are tempted to deceive. It usually stems from simple assumptions—we have a poor excuse and our relationship cannot tolerate the candor. By facing up to these fears, however, we can raise the relationship to a higher level. The student could have used the truth to show he understood that his friendship was solid enough that he could be honest, that he did not have to hold back information.

Imagine the same situation with varied circumstances. Your boss asks you to play golf after work. You would prefer to spend the evening with your family, given that you've recently had little time with your children. You tell your boss you have a lot of work to do, which is true, but you don't really plan to open your briefcase unless you have to. The deception seems like an easy out. But the danger is that it reflects a habit you have developed through mutiple repetitions. The deception is the same as with the student, but the downside even greater.

This does not suggest that truth telling be blunt or biting—calling a jerk a jerk (or a boss insensitive). It means choosing an alternative, skillful way of responding. An old rule of thumb suggests asking ourselves before we speak, Is it true; is it kind; is it useful? If it is not all three, we have not found a skillful way to communicate.[5] This is really another way of saying, Tell the *whole* truth—a truth that takes into account your long-term, mutually beneficial relationship with another person.

Imagine the morning following the comment made to your boss about having too much work to play golf. He asks whether you got your work done. You reply accurately but deceitfully, "Not as much as I would have liked." You begin to see the growing ramifications of your deception. If you had told the truth the evening before, you might now have a truthful conversation about family time—deepening the relationship. But that opportunity is lost, because you never took the time to understand and articulate the whole truth.

As with lying, the temptation to deceive dissipates if we focus on people, not transactions, and keep reciprocity in mind. If we ask someone to a movie, would we want to be lied to? Would we want to second-guess whether our relationship had soured? It's safe to say, most people prefer friends who portray themselves authentically.

One way of recognizing our penchant for a lack of authenticity is to do the "left-column exercise" created by Harvard Business School professor Chris Argyris. Take a blank sheet of paper. Draw a line down the middle. Think about a recent conversation in life, a significant one. In the right column, outline a transcript of the conversation. In the left, note your private thoughts at each point in the conversation.

The exercise highlights how we go through life with two conversations: public and private. Our left column, the private, contains plenty of both worthy and unworthy thoughts. We can strike the unworthy ones. But we can reconsider the worthy. In the television example, our left column might say, "Oh damn, I'm feeling overloaded; I just wanted to be by myself tonight." To the extent we have worthy thoughts, we can move them to the right column. We can practice "no left-column thinking." Articulating our left-column thoughts is another way of making a habit out of finding and expressing the whole truth.

As another example of transformation, consider a story told by a nurse: "I had a colleague who [was dying] of cancer . . . she had a daughter and a son and she had no husband . . . the daughter was not telling her that she was dying . . . [nor] talking to her mother about dying . . . but I couldn't go along with what they wanted . . . because my relationship with that friend was more important than what the daughter and son were wanting, so I went to her this day . . . and said goodbye to her . . . It was just a very privileged moment to be as honest as that and say goodbye, and I think she appreciated it, and I think she'd been surrounded by dishonesty."[6]

The patient died within days. We don't know the truth of her reaction, but we do know that many dying people do not prefer deception. Sissela Bok, author of *Lying*, explains why: "Their concern for knowing about their condition goes far beyond mere curiosity or the wish to make isolated personal choices in the short time left to them; their stance toward the entire life they have lived, and their ability to give it meaning and completion, are at stake."[7]

Though nurses and families often give vague responses and half-truths, and deceive by omission, deception with someone at the end of life damages trust at a time when a dying person may feel most out of control. Even if the motive is to maintain hope, the benefit of the moment comes at a huge cost. Even with a dying person, we can transform relationships for the better.

One of the authors learned this lesson when his stepfather died of lymphoma. Dick was only sixty-eight, a retired veterinarian, a lay pastor, and full of life. When tests confirmed his diagnosis, he had only a few weeks to live. He was sick and scared. The family was tempted to "support" him by focusing on his slim chance of recovery. But his wife overcame her fears and told Dick the whole truth.

An amazing thing happened. As Dick gave his last sermon to his church, he felt hands on his back. He knew he would soon die, but realized he was not alone. Those around him were also afraid, and they needed the help only he could give.

Dick let go of his fear. In his last days, he found deep meaning and purpose in ministering to all those around him. The family thought it was its duty to be strong and supportive. But Dick turned the situation around. He helped his family, his congregation, and even his doctors come to terms with his impending death. After his passing, memories of his final days remained among the family's most precious.

As with lying, we can practice the thinking skills to transcend deception. When we are tempted to nurture misimpressions, omit important facts, and deflect people from the truth, we can instead search for the whole truth, take stock of the people around us, and be honest in the way we would like others to be honest with us.

That doesn't mean we are not diplomatic. We presumably have a genuine desire to be courteous, if not compassionate. As Gandhi is reputed to have said, "Whenever you have truth it must be given with love, or the message and the messenger will be rejected."

Transform Broken Promises

Another temptation to compromise is to break promises. In daily life, people break promises all the time when it suits their prudential needs. Broken promises are often minor, like late payment of small debts, missed dead-lines, skipped appointments, and jobs not done. As with other compro-mises, broken promises often yield a transactional gain at a relationship loss.

We are often tempted to promise something and then back out. We then rationalize—time has erased the obligation, circumstances have changed, we didn't explicitly promise anyway. But however clever our thinking, it doesn't erase compromise.

We can use skillful ethical thinking to turn these temptations into op-portunities. Again, we start with the whole truth. We inform the person to whom we owe the obligation of our need or desire to change. We renegoti-ate the promise with our relationship in mind. And in the spirit of reci-procity, we reaffirm our responsibility for the promise even if it seems stale or forgotten.[8]

Skillful ethical action doesn't require complicated behavior. Are we tempted to break our promise to a neighbor to prune back our overhang-ing apple tree? We talk to the neighbor. Are we tempted to be a deadbeat on a debt to a cousin? Remind the cousin and commit to a feasible time for repayment. Have we missed a deadline? Inform the people depending on us, renegotiate, and reaffirm we will deliver. The commonsense response can transform a relationship.

Some psychologists recommend we apply such principles even to the temptation to break life's most sacred promise: the marriage vow. Are we tempted to infidelity? Before acting, we inform our partner about the temptation of an extramarital affair.[9] The simple act of informing can en-hance the relationship.

A special form of promise is the secret. In our classes, we hear regularly from students plagued with the same secret. Imagine you are such a student: a friend confides in you that he is cheating on his girlfriend. He wants you to keep the infidelity secret. Sooner rather than later, though, his girlfriend asks you about the infidelity. What do you say? Do you keep the secret?

The temptation to reveal the secret is extreme. The lesson in this case is that we all need to be more skilled about accepting secrets in the first place. Here are three criteria for accepting such confidences:

- Make it clear to others that you will not be obligated to keep secret anything you have not been told in advance to keep secret.

- Put a time limit on holding a secret.

- Be clear about the circumstances under which you may disclose the secrets.

Keeping secrets can radically change our relationship with those who might benefit from knowing them, so we must accept them and handle them with care. If a secret is giving us trouble, we can also go back to the person who has taken us into confidence. We can clarify the details of the secret. We can confirm the reciprocity of the agreement. We can commit to a clear time limit. Each of these actions can strengthen the relationship.

Recall the story about one of the author's secrets: not telling his son that he learned the son was about to be laid off. The author didn't reveal the secret, but he could have been more skillful in accepting it in the first place. And he could have been more skillful in going back to his daughter and clarifying the secret, confirming reciprocity, and understanding the time limit.

Secrets receive inordinate attention in daily life. Our ready presumption of their inviolability probably stems from the value we place on loyalty. Loyalty has a strong hold on all of us because it stems from primeval tribal emotions. We are essentially hardwired to think first of kin, clan, caste, and class. We raise arms against others to protect our tribe from interlopers, outsiders, and barbarians. Loyalty, as writer Sissela Bok explains, "precedes law and morality itself . . . it helps assure collective survival in a hostile environment."[10]

Yet we should beware of letting the tug of loyalty preclude our skillful ethical handling of temptations. Loyalty sounds good, but its definition is slippery, and practicing loyalty is not always a virtue. One of the requirements of joining the Mafia is the blood oath—swearing loyalty to the family. But blind allegiance to clan does not necessarily lead to ethical behavior, because loyalty offers no ethical guidance. Whenever someone appeals to our sense of loyalty, we should run the requested behaviors through our ethical filter.

Transform Theft

No less than with lying, deception, and promises, temptations to steal offer opportunities to transform relationships. Sadly, we are easily swayed by small sums to compromise. As observers of others, how often do we marvel at people's sticky fingers? How often do we pocket short-term profits when gains from transcending compromise are much greater?

One of our students related a story about visiting a large home-improvement store to buy a table. To his relief, he arrived just in time to get the last one, for $300. At the checkout, the clerk scanned the bar code, which priced the item at $30. He said nothing and silently blessed his lucky stars at the chain store's error. He paid just $30. Asked in class about the $270 underpayment, he said, "They had it coming."

The student related this anecdote in response to our asking for stories of ethically sensitive situations. He professed a clear conscience, but his explanation suggested otherwise. He deserved the discount, he said, because he was miffed by previous experience with the store's poor-quality goods.

Of course, who could not envy such a fortuitous event? But the question was how to handle it skillfully. He pocketed a nice gain. But what did he do for his relationships—with self, with friends, with classmates, with local merchants? The pricing error was a financial opportunity but also an ethical one. What would he have done if he had searched for the whole truth, weighed alternatives to improve relationships, and factored in the reciprocity of, say, the Golden Rule?

If he had done so, he might have made a decision that rewarded him less in terms of dollars and cents and more in character and relationships. To be sure, many students might rib him about his stupidity. Who wouldn't take the money and run? The same might be said of the individual who underpaid $17 on his restaurant tab in chapter 1. But who trusts such people? Friends? Siblings? Parents? Theft of all kinds corrodes relationships.

One temptation to steal that requires especially skillful ethical handling is accepting something that is not rightfully ours—as did Paul Hamm in the story of accepting a 2004 Olympic medal he won owing to a scoring error. A woman who illustrates how Hamm could have done otherwise is Irina Karavaeva, a Russian gymnast who won the Olympic gold medal in Sydney in 2000 in the individual trampoline competition.[11]

Karavaeva competes under the umbrella of the International Gymnastics Federation (FIG), the same organization as Hamm. In 2001, at the World Championships competition in Denmark, Karavaeva faced precisely the same situation as Hamm in 2004. By virtue of a scoring computation error, discovered later, she erroneously received the gold medal. But Karavaeva didn't resort to legal action to retain the gold, which she was under no obligation to relinquish. Upon learning of the mistake, she asked the FIG to grant the medal to Anna Dogonadze, the German silver medal winner.

Karavaeva, who then exchanged medals with Dogonadze, said it was just a matter of justice. Karavaeva went on to compete against Dogonadze in the next Olympics in 2004 in Athens, where Dogonadze won the gold. Karavaeva lost in the preliminaries, but she had already attracted global attention the year before. In Paris, the United Nations honored her, with Secretary-General Kofi Annan present, with an award for fair play. She won plaudits for her exemplary conduct in the practice of sport.

Such acts show the power of transcending temptation. We don't have to compete in the Olympics to discover such opportunities. Recall the vignette of the three students who each borrowed, in succession, a wide-screen television at no charge for ninety days. Each had alternatives available that would have yielded relationship gains far in excess of financial ones.

And what about the coach of the University of Colorado football team, who embraced the error by referees to win a key game with the University of Missouri? Colorado coach Bill McCartney, who later expressed his regret at the decision, surely learned that winning a game is one thing; winning in his role of setting a good example of building character and relationships is another.

When we are tempted to filch small items, appropriate office supplies, download copyrighted works, accept (or give) bribes, steal items from "anonymous" owners and "big" companies, and profit from others' ignorance and mistakes, we can halt our actions. We can ask ourselves, Is this how we want others to treat us? How would we act to transform the situation if we used skillful ethical decision making?

Transform Harm

Temptations to harm make up the last significant opportunity to turn potential compromise to our advantage. If we are a soldier, we may face a conundrum like one of our student's. In his second tour in Iraq in 2006, he was coming under fire while half a dozen people were running in front of the sniper shooting at him. He could put his crosshairs on the sniper. But he had to decide: do I pull the trigger and possibly hit civilians? Since he would not take a chance of killing innocents, he held his fire.

In most of our personal lives, we don't face such temptations to kill or harm. We are more likely to come across situations where our *inaction* could cause harm, or where actions connect us to harm through one or more degrees of separation. Years ago, a woman in Silicon Valley was arrested for not paying her taxes. She refused because a small portion of them supported war. A reporter asked her why she brought such trouble on herself. Her response: in the time of gas ovens, I could not have bought one brick.[12]

The question of how to transform a situation when it involves some degree of separation is often unclear, even if we take a skillful approach to thinking. One case that makes this point is "The Parable of the Sadhu," by Bowen McCoy, a classic *Harvard Business Review* case.[13] McCoy tells the story of how, a number of years ago, in the Himalaya range in Asia, he was climbing to a high pass, around 18,000 feet. He and his group were in a rush to cross because they had a small window of time while conditions were safe. Ahead of them on the trail was a party of New Zealanders, behind a party of Japanese.

As they climbed, a New Zealander staggered down with a man slung over his shoulders. The man was a pilgrim, a *sadhu*, an Indian holy man, who had collapsed, shivering, on the ice. He was semiconscious, wore tattered clothes, was unable to walk. He didn't even have shoes. He must have been returning from Muklinath, an ancient holy place for pilgrims. When he reached the pass, he must have succumbed to the cold and to altitude sickness—for which the only cure is rapid descent to the valley.

McCoy and his party set to work. They clothed the man, fed him liquids, revived him, and gave him directions for descending. As they worried about the weather deteriorating, they then trekked onward. They did not miss perhaps their only opportunity in a lifetime to get through the pass. As for the sadhu, the last people across the pass reported he was resting on a rock where they had left him, not yet walking, listlessly throwing rocks at a hiker's dog.

Was their action toward the sadhu ethical? McCoy's hiking companion criticized their decision when he arrived at the pass. He maintained that, with the sadhu still at 15,000 feet, they may have contributed to his death—although nobody knew for sure. As armchair observers, we can say that McCoy probably did the "right" thing, even went one step beyond the right thing. After all, he reached out and saved someone from certain death.

We could all encounter a situation just like that of McCoy's. It could happen after an auto accident or on a stroll down the sidewalk when we pass a homeless person. Like McCoy, we would consider our action (or inaction) ethical or unethical depending on our personal ethical code. In McCoy's case, we don't know for sure how he felt, but we can clearly say he stopped short of his potential to turn the episode into an opportunity for transformation. He was faced with a chance to make a sacrifice for another, to be a hero, even. The question lingers: was he offered a chance at one of life's most enriching experiences, and did he let it slip through his fingers?

McCoy suggests he realizes he did let an opportunity pass. He notes that, when he had altitude sickness himself six years earlier, Nepalese locals took him into their home for five days to recover. It was his most memorable experience in Nepal, and we can speculate that it was a transformative experience for his hosts.

If we are to pose some of the questions of skillful ethical decision making, we can ask, Did he clearly understand the whole truth of his relationship to the sadhu? Could he have better focused on relationships to improve his choice of alternatives? Did he amply explore the issue of reciprocity reflected in the metal rules?

If only to contrast with McCoy's experience, consider again John Rabe. We can speculate that Rabe grasped right away the whole truth of the situation, that he considered alternatives that took into account relationships with all stakeholders, and that he operated clearly in tune with the reciprocity of at least the Golden Rule. He more than transcended temptation, and he transformed himself and others.

The closing chapter in the Rabe story shows just how much. After the war, in 1948, the people of Nanking learned that Rabe had fallen into poverty. He and his family were destitute. They took up a collection and sent him $2,000. Nanking's mayor meanwhile shipped to Rabe four huge packages of food: sausages, tea, coffee, butter, jam. In Berlin, the Rabe family had been reduced to eating wild weeds with soup, and the kind acts restored Rabe's faith in life.[14]

Most of us do not expect (or even desire) saintly behavior, but we can better tap into ethical opportunities that arise from temptations to harm. This is true even if they are as simple as the temptation by a smoker to subject his or her family to secondhand smoke. Or as gut wrenching as a son or daughter asked by a parent with a terminal illness to assist in his or her suicide. In either case, we can practice ethical thinking skills to take better advantage. If we are tempted to harm others to prevent a greater harm, or ignore our imposition of risk on others, or ignore harm beyond what we can see, or support harm indirectly, we can give extra thought to our actions.

One of the actions related to harm that raises the most debate is reproductive choice. Do we have questions about the ethics of abortion, surrogate motherhood, sperm donation, egg donation, or the promise of stem cell or embryonic stem cell research? Choosing transformative alternatives calls not so much for new skills but for a focused application of the same ones. Each of us has to make our own choices according to our own ethical principles.

The Growth Choice

In answer to many ethical challenges, only one simple, obvious choice is appropriate. Not all situations allow a variety of alternatives. But sometimes we have many good alternatives, and then what do we do? In a sense, we face the option of selecting a "growth choice." We choose our actions according to our capacity for personal and interpersonal growth. The level of choice—and challenge—is up to us.

If we are looking for a place to get started on the road to growth, we would do well to focus on practicing the skills of transformation through telling the whole truth. We can ask, What is the full scope of this temptation? Have I carefully sorted prudential issues from ethical ones? What are the actions I can choose to respond wisely? Have I fully considered reciprocity?

The power of the truth to transform reflects the power of ethics as a whole to transform. In a self-discovery session attended by one of the authors, a participant, a father, told how his terminally ill son filled the spaces in his coloring books by using only one crayon: the black one. The father was in anguish. He could not tell his son he was going to die, or how aggrieved he was.

A week later, the father returned to another session. He had finally gotten to the truth with his son. He told him that life was short, that he loved him, and he would miss him. A barrier seemed to fall. The truth straightened and deepened the relationship. His son returned to his coloring books, but this time his approach was not dark: he used crayons of every color.

The truth transforms. And so do choices to transcend temptations to steal and harm. As we will discuss in the next chapter, selecting the growth choice transforms not just our personal lives. It has a special way to transform our work lives as well.

➤ Your Turn: Transform Daily Life

Choose a decision from your life that fell into the gray area of ethics. Now use the three skills highlighted in this chapter to rethink how you could have acted had you been more skillful: Clarify the whole truth. Frame the situation as one of relationships. Ask how you would have treated a loved one. What alternatives could/should you have considered to transform the situation into an opportunity to strengthen relationships with others?

CHAPTER 7

Transform Work

Skillful Decision Making in the Workplace

Virtue is bold, and goodness never fearful.

—William Shakespeare[1]

WHEN THE BOTTOM FELL OUT of the dot-com market at the turn of the century, Outcome Software was hit hard. Although the start-up firm had raised $10 million in venture capital, cash was running out. Venture capitalists, eager to earn back their money, intervened. They asked the founder and COO to keep the looming financial crisis to himself, lest the firm lose key software engineers to other, more secure companies.[2]

But the COO, an author of this book, decided not to take part in this deception. From the point of view of the venture capitalists, the act of telling employees the full truth—that a funding crisis jeopardized their future paychecks—deprived the firm of an extra chance of success. It was better to wait until the last moment so people wouldn't look for other jobs.

The COO told the venture capitalists otherwise. Maybe they *should* start looking for other jobs, he said, because that's a decision they need to make for themselves.

The COO had already experienced the power of telling the whole truth as a way to transform relationships with his employees. When he was CEO during the start-up's early years, before venture funding, he would occasionally run short of cash. Each month, he talked openly with employees about financials, sales prospects, and if necessary, the possibility nobody would get paid.

The policy in case of a cash flow squeeze was explicit: if the company didn't have enough money for payroll, the founders would not take salary for the first month, the rest of the leadership team would join them in the second month, and if the problem persisted, all employees would go without salary in the third month. Three times in three years, he had to invoke the paycheck-freeze policy, once lasting for four months.

But through it all, only one out of a dozen people quit (a single mother). Instead of undercutting relationships with others, telling the whole truth, though scary, strengthened team bonds. Successfully weathering three financial storms together built tremendous loyalty. People felt they were building the business together; everyone felt a sense of ownership.

The COO's actions show how businesspeople can go beyond doing the right thing. The COO could have followed a policy of keeping financial conditions and sales prospects confidential. If he had made that an explicit practice, it certainly would have been ethical. He chose a more creative alternative: to be open and transparent. In essence, he based his ethical approach on the same elements stressed in the last chapter. He searched for the whole truth inside himself, created alternatives that stressed stakeholder relationships, and raised the reciprocity bar to treat others as he would himself.

There Is Only One You

Despite stories of this kind, a misunderstanding persists in the field of ethics—that people should practice "business ethics" at work and "personal ethics" at home. In the story about Outcome, we might ask, Why did the COO feel any responsibility to avoid deception of employees? In business, the axiom is caveat emptor, "let the buyer beware." Wasn't it the employees' responsibility to figure out their future? Besides, in a start-up company, shouldn't employees realize their company could go out of business fast?

The notion of a double standard comes from an error in thinking, that situations, rather than our inner voice, dictate our actions. As we learned in chapter 2, we can easily fall into the double-standard trap. We put on prison-guard uniforms, and (without thinking and training) we adopt the demeanor of brutish guards. We put on clothes for the workplace, commute to work, and we accept our boss's permission to cut corners.

If we look beyond situations, however, we see that *all* ethics are personal. We use decision-making standards that are personal. We affect other people personally. Our actions reflect on us as persons. We cultivate only one kind of integrity: personal.

Work does pose special challenges and constraints, whether we're faced with lying, deceiving, stealing, or harming. We all have bosses, to whom we feel we should defer. We are compelled to focus on numbers, which divert attention from people. We rely on teams to succeed, which put us at the mercy of peer pressure and groupthink. But our actions still depend on the ethics of the same person inside.

We often do not feel free to exercise our personal ethics. In fact, our professions or organizations may call on us to follow ethical rules that diverge from our own. We may even feel pressure to violate our personal code and rationalize our behavior by citing "the way things work" in business or government or politics or civic organizations.

That's why one of life's weightiest decisions is what to do for a living. What trade or profession do we enter? What organization do we work in? If we are to end each day without compromising, we want to join an organization that is compatible with our principles.

The Right Profession

As in our personal lives, the wisest course of action is often to avoid ethically sensitive situations in the first place. A number of questions are helpful in finding a trade or profession that fits us ethically:

- Are we comfortable with the temptations we would face in this job?

- How do the people in the profession behave when faced with temptation?

- Do enough degrees of separation stand between us and objectionable actions?

- Do we want to be like the people at the top of this profession? Given that leaders set the tone, are they ethical role models?

For an illustration of the thinking needed, let's look in detail at just the first question: are we comfortable with the temptations in the profession? Before we choose to be a lawyer, for example, we can ask whether we are ready for one of the more onerous aspects of the profession: keeping secrets. The legal profession requires an extreme level of secrecy. Spouses, whose lives are very much affected by what the attorneys do, are not privy to their work.

Keeping some secrets may also be ethically uncomfortable. Imagine an in-house attorney reporting to a CEO, who, against the attorney's advice, engages in legally risky behavior. In so doing, the CEO's actions may violate the personal ethics of the attorney and put not only the CEO, but the company and the attorney, in legal jeopardy. What does the dissenting attorney do?

The situation puts the attorney in a bind. While he or she may take great personal offense at the CEO's actions, and may even be at great personal risk, the attorney is duty-bound to be a zealous advocate for and achieve the best results under the law for the client. An attorney is a fiduciary. This means the attorney is duty-bound to act in the client's best interest even if it is not in the attorney's best interest. This positive ethic goes far beyond the negative ethic of doctors to simply "do no harm." In most jurisdictions, blowing the whistle on bad behavior is out of the question. An attorney could not turn in the CEO even if the actions contemplated involved death or injury to another.

In law firms, another issue arises. In Silicon Valley, for example, lawyers routinely ask clients to waive conflicts of interest, because firms advise high-tech companies on many levels, often representing competitors. Bound to keep vital secrets, the attorneys are forced to distinguish between general insights and company-specific information. Passing information obtained from one client to another, to the detriment of the first, is unethical. Attorneys in such a closely knit legal community face this dilemma regularly.

Other professions pose similarly tough ethical temptations. Consider a physician whose male patient tests positive for the AIDS virus. The physician can urge the patient to tell his wife but cannot say anything himself, even if the wife is one of his patients. Suppose the physician sees the wife at the local country club. What does he say? We can debate what is right or wrong, but we can also choose to anticipate such ethical binds and, if uncomfortable, forgo joining this particular profession.

Similar conflicts arise in other professions. Law enforcement officers are often obliged to lie if they do undercover work. Engineers may feel obliged to overlook harm if it means admitting corporate liability for faulty products. Journalists may feel obliged to engage in deception to obtain information from difficult sources. If we are considering these jobs, we will want to be comfortable with the specific ethical challenges that they entail.

The Right Affiliation

In the same way that trades and professions pose ethical challenges, so does every organization, and even every industry. To be ethically content in our work life, we need to vet an organization before we join. If we do not, sooner or later, we will wish we did. Only 56 percent of U.S. workers define their current company as having an ethical culture, according to surveys by consulting firm LRN.[3]

While we can't really know the ethics until we join, we can watch for tip-offs to the ethical standards of a company. One red flag is the questionable behavior of people. As in a profession, the tone at the top shapes the culture we will work in day in and day out. Are the top executives or managers role models? Will spending time with them bring out the best in us? If we are not comfortable with the choices made by our boss or our boss's boss, we may find it fruitful to ask more questions about the organization.

Another red flag is the organization's ethical code, especially if it puts emphasis on obeying the law. The law is a minimum standard, not necessarily a desirable one. (In fact, obeying the law may be a prudential practice rather than an ethical one.) Companies focused solely on legal compliance, as opposed to answering to an independent ethical benchmark, are more likely to compromise ethics for profit. This is especially true when they are following laws that free peoples consider unethical, like the censorship laws in China.

A third potential red flag is conflicts in everyday business practices. A company may strictly enforce a prohibition on the release of any confidential information (but what if your customer is about to buy an obsolete product, and you would prefer to be honest?); or prohibit speaking ill of competitors (but what if the competitor produces a dangerous product?); or allow gifts of certain specified amounts (but what if the company allows gifts of amounts that cross our line for bribery?). We have to decide for ourselves whether these issues conflict with our ethics, and if so, we must avoid these organizations.

Organizations in some industries—tobacco, firearms, security, nuclear power, advertising, and others—may raise other ethical red flags, depending on our personal ethical code. What are the practices in these industries, and how close do they come to lying, stealing, and harming? For an extreme example, suppose we are thinking of joining the CIA. If we take a job as a spy, we need to be prepared to lie (if not steal and harm). The same is true for an undercover police officer. If we take a job as a soldier, we have to be prepared to kill when ordered to do so. It goes with the territory.

If we wake up to an ethically uncomfortable environment, we face the tough choice of whether to leave an organization. This obviously is not easy. But it's a question many of us may face. A remarkable 36 percent of workers in the U.S. say they have left a job because they disagreed with a company's ethical standards.[4] The lesson is that as we ponder a job offer, it is useful to include an ethical evaluation. Our character, our relationships, and certainly our satisfaction with the job all depend on it.

Transform Lying at Work

We may well view lying at work as a practical, even clever, tool. Small lies in particular—told to bosses, customers, colleagues, investors, regulators—may seem to be acceptable indiscretions and not foul play. They are the feints and head fakes of the work world. But whether we lie to earn a few brownie points over a colleague or to win a million-dollar order at the expense of a competitor, we make the same sacrifice we do in our personal lives. We gain in the transaction while losing in relationships.

We also miss the opportunity to transform the temptation. Recall the vignette from chapter 1 in which we imagined ourselves as a consultant who bids $200,000 for a $300,000 job. We figure our client will eventually agree to the necessary extra work and expense anyway, so why put the project at risk by bidding the full amount? The reason we fib is that we fear there is no alternative to lying.

But again, we always have alternatives to lying. We can explore them by asking the same kinds of questions we would ask in our personal lives: What is the whole truth about our intentions and desires and fears? What creative alternatives come to mind when we think first about the relationship? How could we reshape our behavior if guided by a stronger sense of reciprocity, by the Golden, platinum, diamond, or other metal rules?

The whole truth might have been this: "In our best professional judgment, the work will ultimately require $300,000 for completion. There is an incentive for us to bid low, only $200,000, so that we could win the bid. We would then have you committed to the project, and you would probably agree to added work and cost later. But we prefer to bid the job fully loaded up front. We know this encourages you to take your business elsewhere, but we don't want to get our relationship started on the wrong foot."

By taking this approach, we would have to recognize why we considered lying in the first place—namely, that we didn't trust our customer to value our work or value the truth. By addressing this issue, we change the question from Is this an ethical transaction? to Is this the way we want to work with our client? Focused on a person, rather than a purchase order, we can build for the long term.

Note that if we take a consequence-based approach to ethics, we can fall into several of the traps described earlier in the book. One trap is excusing untruths because we feel a higher purpose justifies it—for example, lying to a client to save our business's reputation or lying to maintain cash flow to pay employees. But excuses can drive us into all kinds of ethically questionable behavior, as we see regularly in business, government, politics, the nonprofit sector, and elsewhere.

In journalism, reporters sometimes earn praise by obtaining access to documents or people through ruses. The gains in these individual transactions (translating into juicy stories) may well pale in comparison to the loss of public confidence in journalists. In the Gallup organization's annual surveys of trust in professions, journalists rank in the bottom tier.[5] No surprise that people routinely distrust journalists and stymie their inquiries.

In the nonprofit sector, one manager who demonstrated how to transform a lying culture is Charles Anderson, CEO of the United Way of the

National Capital Area in Washington, D.C. Anderson took over the local United Way in 2003, after the jailing of former CEO Oral Suer for fraud. Anderson was faced with rebuilding donors' trust in the organization, and he chose radical transparency and accountability to do so.[6]

Anderson took his job in July 2003, just six weeks before the release of a forensic audit of past misdeeds. In his job interview, the board asked him how he would handle the audit's bad news. "I'd take that sucker and put it right on the web," he recalls saying. "Let the whole world read the good, the bad, and the ugly about this organization." The audit released damning truths about former practices, like cashing in annual vacation and sick leave, paying for expenses without receipts, disbursing pension payments in advance, and reimbursing the former CEO for his own charitable pledges.

The report concluded the United Way affiliate had been looted of roughly $1.5 million. The organization needed a radical transformation. Two-thirds of the forty-five-person staff left or were eliminated by Anderson. Anderson then opened all of the organization's files to the public, except confidential donor and personnel records. In a rare move for a charity, the chapter chose to voluntarily comply with the appropriate provisions of the Sarbanes-Oxley Act of 2002, including some of the costly Section 404 internal controls procedures aimed at preventing fraud in corporations.

Anderson's efforts stabilized donations, which had plunged by two-thirds after the earlier scandal. He continued to use relentless candor to bring back donors. When he was accused in 2006 by his own chief financial officer of misstating sums raised in the 2004–2005 campaign, he ended a long-running practice of using projected rather than actual contribution figures—even though it was and remains standard elsewhere in the United Way system.

Like all managers, Anderson ran the risk that candor would give critics ammunition to attack him. The *Washington Post* did so—challenging his integrity for using the projected figures.[7] The newspaper called the practice a "stumble." But Anderson's candor defused talk of misconduct and simply led to stronger relationships with stakeholders. As proof, the number of new company donors rose from under 100 in 2005–2006 to 176 in 2006–2007. His 2006–2007 campaign chair asked to stay on for a second year and joined the board of directors. In a town that reveres its local football franchise, the Washington Redskins, quarterback Jason Campbell signed on as a United Way pitchman.

Today in workplaces everywhere, managers instruct people to "do the right thing" or "do things right." They give integrity top billing in speeches and newsletters. But their efforts may actually encourage people to sell the potential of ethics short, to use ethical principles as ground rules, not as powerful levers to transform relations among individuals, groups, and organizations. As Anderson and other managers show, truth telling and transparency are the basis for a new way of managing people.

Truth-telling alternatives that transform relationships have much more power than calculated "harmless" lies. If we find ourselves tempted to exaggerate in interviews, to lie to underlings in performance reviews, to use half-truths in marketing, to cheat on facts and figures, to puff up reports to investors, we can stop. We can search for the whole truth and find honest ways to express ourselves candidly, transparently, the way we would like others to—and build stronger bonds with others in the long run.

"Always tell the truth," as the old saying goes. "It will amaze your friends and astound your enemies." And we could add that this works in the workplace as well as in personal life.[8]

Transform Deception at Work

To many people, deception at work is another compromise that seems to be justified by the situation. Who, for instance, hasn't felt the urge to engage in the dance of deceit so common in buying or selling a car? We associate mistruths with smooth-tongued used-car salesmen (who rank even below journalists in the Gallup trust index), but we can all get easily drawn into the apparent advantages of a deceit-filled used-car transaction.

But these temptations again offer opportunities to act in a beneficial way instead. Recall that one of our students told the story of preparing for an international trade show. The student's company had invented a software program to solve standard problems twice as fast as a competitor's software. To show this off, the company designed a demonstration pitting its software head-to-head against its competitor's.

But just before the show, a technical problem unrelated to the software made the simultaneous competition impossible. Company managers, however, asked the student to run the demonstration anyway, using files from earlier sessions to make it *appear* that the software worked. The engineer was not to reveal the fakery—and he didn't.

Now what would have happened if the engineer, instead of caving into his boss's pressure, had insisted on honesty? What if he had said, "Look boss, this really makes me uncomfortable. I like to think of myself as the kind of person who tells the truth, and I like to think of this organization as one that tells the truth." How would that have changed his relations with his boss? Perhaps an irate boss would fire him or sideline him, but if he worked in an honest company, his comment would certainly come across as a wake-up call.

Temptations to deceive at work come with extra complexity. We are not in a position to control what others do. We work in teams where it's hard to act unilaterally. And we know that if we don't compromise, someone else often will. That then raises the degrees-of-separation question: Do we share culpability for compromises committed at arm's length (or cubicle's width)? How can we be sure the transgression is not too close for us to look the other way?

In a true story from the food industry, looking the other way had become a tradition. The chairman of a small frozen-vegetable company learned soon after taking her post that well water used to wash vegetables in her plant was contaminated by toluene, benzene, and xylene. A plume of tainted water had migrated onto the company's land, and into its wells, from a dry cleaner and nearby petroleum tanks. Despite the contamination, the plant was still shipping product to longtime customers in the institutional and baby-food markets. The previous executives had looked the other way.[9]

The temptation to continue to ignore the issue was strong for many in the company. The plant manager tried to persuade the chairman that the parts-per-billion pollutant levels were too small to matter, and that the contaminants probably volatilized during processing anyway. But nobody knew whether the thousands of pounds of frozen product already in the warehouse were clean. All they knew was that customers, who usually tested incoming product, were not complaining.

The chairman could have continued to run the plant and not tell customers, but instead issued an edict: nothing gets shipped until we review the problem with counsel and test the product for pollutants. Her first legal counsel continued to nurse the temptation to feign ignorance. When he came with several associates to speak at a senior managers' meeting, he presented the chairman with two options. "The first we call the ostrich technique," he began.

The chairman chuckled to herself and then hired another law firm. This time, one of the firm's partners talked directly to an official in the U.S. Department of Agriculture. The advice this time: Intensively test the product in the warehouse for each of the specific chemicals to determine whether it is clean. If it is, ship it.

The transformative effect of her decision, though hardly complex, was hard to understate. Every manager and employee knew the new chairman was serious about ending a history of sloppy quality and deliberately ignoring potential problems. Her decision transmitted a message through the whole organization: the water isn't testing right, and if we don't figure out how to get a new system, we're not shipping product.

This approach reinforced the focus of her entire tenure. As she often reminded employees, "Our goal is to make a good company better." Making decisions to jeopardize quality was going in the wrong direction.

In the same way as in our personal lives, when we are tempted to omit facts, deflect people from the truth, use evasive or euphemistic language, or deceive in any number of ways, we can instead stop to reflect. We can explore the whole truth of our intentions, factor the concerns of stakeholders into our decisions, and come up with an approach that shows equitable, reciprocal, and virtuous behavior. In the case of the freezing plant, the product tested clean, and about four days later the company resumed shipments. Meanwhile, it shut down its wells and ran a new main to municipal water.

The effect of choosing creative, ethical alternatives has much broader impact than just doing things right. In the final chapter of the story about Outcome Software, when the COO was unsuccessful in talking the venture capitalists out of their plans to keep finances secret, the COO quit. He refused to treat his employees in this way. He did not consider his resignation a transformational alternative, but at least it did not violate his ethics. One year later, Outcome closed down. But eventually his earlier actions came back to help him. When he launched another start-up three years later, many of the people formerly at Outcome joined the new company.

Transform Broken Promises at Work

The temptation at work to indulge in another form of deception—to break promises and commitments—arises with every deadline, every deliverable, every dollar budgeted or spent. While we faithfully intend to tell other people what we will do, and other people expect us to do what we say, our discipline invariably wavers. We get caught compromising.

To minimize ethical problems with commitments, we will find it useful to understand the concept of a "quality" commitment.[10] A commitment is an agreement between two people, whom we will call the "requester" and the "promisor." If we break the process down, a commitment has four steps: a request (from requester to promisor), a promise (from promisor to requester), delivery (from promisor to requester), and acceptance (from requester to promisor).

A "quality" request requires the requester and the promisor to share a background understanding of the situation. The requester and the promisor jointly agree that the promisor has the knowledge, skills, resources, and time to fulfill the commitment. They clearly establish the conditions of satisfaction, in terms of timing, quality, and quantity.

A "poor quality" commitment can arise when these conditions are not met. If a breakdown in a commitment comes from lack of skill or sloppy management, the breakdown is unfortunate, but not unethical. A request that a promisor cannot refuse is not part of a quality commitment; it is an order. An order may seem unfair or unwise, but it's not unethical to issue one. The commitment must be owned by both parties, but the order is owned by just one.

If the breakdown comes from our purposely setting up a poor-quality commitment, the breakdown raises ethical questions. The most obvious compromise in a commitment comes when a promisor is not committed to the promise. But also common are situations in which requesters, particularly busy bosses, fail to be committed to the requests they make. Both are common deceptions. To avoid these transgressions, a quality commitment must include both a quality request and a quality promise.

We may think that an ethical compromise is unavoidable when we realize we simply cannot make good on our commitments. But as with other ethical challenges, we have alternatives. If we think we cannot honor commitments, we don't have to simply let them go. We can use the challenge as a signal to try to transform relationships instead.

A simple technique too often gets overlooked: ask the people with whom we made the commitment what they think. The act of renegotiation is an opportunity to build an even stronger relationship. This principle works the same as in our personal lives.

Transform Temptations to Keep (and Reveal) Secrets

Commitments to keep secrets are among the most difficult to maintain. Here again, to minimize ethical problems, we can develop a habit of making secrets carefully—letting other parties know we won't keep secrets except by agreeing to do so beforehand, putting time limits on secrets, and clarifying conditions for keeping them. If we feel pressed to reveal the secret, we can clarify the secret with the requester, reaffirm time limits, and confirm our reciprocal responsibilities.

One effective tool for managing secrets is to make an explicit secrets agreement with the requester. For example: "I agree not to tell your secrets for x years, and you understand that I have made the same promise to others and that I will not disclose their secrets to you, no matter how helpful those secrets might be to you. If a situation arises in which I cannot do my best work because of this understanding on secrecy, I will withdraw from the project."

Imagine you are a consulting engineer on a project for Alpha Company. You are asked to analyze and improve Alpha's portfolio of research projects. One of the projects is a new chemical, J-22, that promises to double the yield of any agricultural crop at very low cost. In your development and commercialization analysis for the chemical, you find an obscure technical paper that reveals a fundamental flaw in the chemistry, a flaw that cannot be overcome. Reluctantly, you recommend that Alpha abandon J-22, and you finish your work on the portfolio without it.

A year later, you lead a research portfolio project for Beta Company. In the middle of your work, the client tells you they have come up with a great new project to add to the portfolio. They have discovered a chemical, J-22, which appears to double agricultural yields. They want you to fast-track its development. What do you do?

One alternative is to say, "I examined that for another company, and it will not work." But you have promised to keep Alpha Company's secrets, and Alpha paid you lots of money to find out that J-22 is flawed.

A second alternative is to call Alpha and say, "I am working for one of your competitors, and they think that J-22 is a great idea. Is it OK if I tell them that it is not?" Alpha might well say, "No! We prefer to see our competitors wasting their money rather than spending it on things that might hurt our business."

A third alternative is to say nothing and keep working. Beta Company may or may not discover the flaw in J-22. Either way, you will be wasting their money. Even worse, if Beta does not find out about the defect, you are going to be wasting an ever greater amount of funds with each passing day.

A fourth alternative is to tell Beta Company that for reasons you cannot explain you will withdraw from the project and arrange for a trusted, capable colleague to take over. You will also absorb the cost of bringing your colleague (who has no knowledge about J-22) up to speed. The situation may remain awkward, but you withdraw yourself from both breaking the secret and setting up an ongoing deception.

To see why you might follow this last path, imagine that the presidents of the two companies are playing golf together a few years later. Suppose that Beta Company proceeded with J-22 and then took a huge write-off, a blunder publicized by the local paper. The president of Alpha Company, Alice, says to the president of Beta, Barbara, "You took quite a loss on J-22." Barbara replies, "Yes, we did." Alice says, "You don't know this, but we looked into J-22 just before you did and found it was a turkey."

Now imagine how the conversation would go after the presidents discover your role at both companies. If you had stayed with the project at Beta Company, you can imagine Barbara saying, "Robin didn't say anything about the problem with J-22. I can't believe we paid him for wasting our money!" She then feels taken advantage of. But you left the project, so Barbara actually says, "Robin started as our project leader, too. I guess I now understand why he withdrew just as we were getting into J-22." Barbara feels chagrined.

In the work world, handling of secrets can pose many other unique temptations of this kind. Suffice it to say that with effort we can come up with creative alternatives that allow us both to keep the secret and to advance our relationships in an ethical way.

Transform Theft at Work

When it comes to temptations to steal at work, we often rely on legalistic reasoning to draw the line between acquiring something fairly and acquiring something through ethically gray means. We defer to tax law, accounting rules, securities regulation, gifting policy, and property-handling rules. If we can't find a law, rule, regulation, or policy that says something is not ours, we help ourselves.

In chapter 1, we imagined ourselves as consultants on a flight to visit a client. We billed the client for the entire travel time. We also billed several hours to another client for work we did on the plane. No rule or law prohibits double billing. But we sense this is ethically gray. If we are to transform this situation, we ask, What is the whole truth of the matter? What would a creative alternative look like if we took into account the interests of our stakeholders (clients)? How would we expect to be billed if we were the client?

By answering these questions, we may come up with more interesting alternatives. What if we asked our client what he or she thought? We could create an opportunity to strengthen a relationship, an opportunity we would probably lose by double billing without our client's awareness. Once again, we could resist reaping a transactional gain at a relationship loss.

Or consider an example in an even grayer area. We are the proprietor of a hardware store. An elderly woman comes to the cash register with an expensive carpenter's hammer. We ask, "Did you find what you need?" She replies, "I found the perfect hammer to hang my pictures." Many cheaper hammers for household tasks can be found in the store. Do we inquire whether she might want to make a less costly purchase? Or do we just take her money?

The question is, Is it stealing to take advantage of her ignorance? It may or may not be, depending on our ethical code. But in any case, we face an opportunity to transcend our code, and in turn transform a relationship: we can recommend a different hammer, save the woman money, and probably secure her enduring goodwill.

Stories in the media often play on the theme of building goodwill with others by transforming temptations to steal. The people who resist temptation can become instant role models. In 2007, New York taxi driver Osman Chowdhury discovered a bag left in his trunk by a previous passenger. It contained thirty diamond rings and a laptop computer, worth over $30,000. With the help of the Taxi Workers' Alliance, and multiple phone calls, he found the owner (a woman who no doubt regretted having tipped him just $0.30 on a $10.70 ride).[11]

Upon returning the bag, Chowdhury accepted only a $100 reward. Media worldwide, including the BBC, then ran stories about his actions. The New York City Taxi and Limousine Commission gave him an award. The city council of New York gave him a citation for his honesty. Even members of the Bangladeshi community in New York spoke out, expressing pride in a fellow immigrant. Such can be the power of transforming a simple temptation to steal.

We encounter less glamorous temptations all the time at work. When we face such situations, we have alternatives to forgo the tempting financial gain and instead reap more enduring gains in relationships. When we are tempted to engage in creative accounting, aggressive legal tactics, intellectual property infringement, appropriation of supplies from our organizations, we can think again. We can ask, What other choices are there?

Transform Harm at Work

Temptations to harm in the workplace arise far more often than many of us like to admit. Even if we do not personally face temptations, we live in a global economy where our efforts often intersect with those of others who do. Makers of unhealthful or harmful products, firms engaged in child labor, units of rogue foreign regimes, units of our own government, corporations profiting from harm in their global operations, advocacy groups tainted by violence, firms engaged in objectionable scientific research—many of these organizations connect with our lives.

The question is not so much whether we will harm another in our presence. It's a question of how many degrees of separation are between us and the harm, and how ethically sensitive we decide we will be. Once again, we have to ask, How close is too close to take action? Even if we leave military service aside, we may face decisions about whether to share culpability at work for harming others.

Suppose we are an engineer for I. A. Topf and Sons in the 1940s, and we have just received a contract for making gas ovens. Is this too close?

Suppose we are a military contractor and we receive a contract to make land mines used around the world? Or rifles? Or night-vision goggles? Or suppose we are the baker asked to supply donuts to concentration-camp guards.

Consider another kind of situation. We are mutual fund managers. Is it OK to put I. A. Topf and Sons in our portfolio? Or suppose we are mutual fund advisors. Is it OK to recommend a mutual-fund manager who has I. A. Topf and Sons in his firm's portfolio? Again, how close is too close? How big do we want our ethical space to be?

In chapter 1 we imagined we were an ophthalmologist, and we repeatedly encountered patients whose previous eye surgery was botched by a colleague. We took no action on the harm. That is, we did not report the colleague, nor did any of our peers. But let's look at that case again. We could have searched for the full truth of the situation: Though loyal to a peer by protecting him from a damaged career, we could have acknowledged we were just one degree of separation from his harm. We could have asked, Is that too close? Are we complicit in a once-removed sort of way? Depending on our codes, we may well be.

In every profession, the issue of exposing incompetent peers is taboo. No one wants to out the charlatans of our own kind. But our ethical codes could oblige us to take action. As in the case of the ophthalmologist, we can search for creative alternatives. Perhaps we could form a consensus with colleagues to steer only simple cases to the mediocre professional while insisting he enroll in remedial training.

Myriad other cases come up in the workplace. If we are a pharmacist who rejects abortion, do we fill a prescription for an abortion pill? If we are a lab technician and scientists begin building weapons, do we stick with our job even if it violates our personal beliefs? If we are a salesperson in a drug company that downplays the cardiovascular side effects of a new drug, do we elevate the question to higher authority? If we are a military lawyer asked to try a defendant who was tortured to produce evidence, do we stay with the case?

When we are tempted to ignore harm within a couple of degrees of separation, or tempted to put others at risk, or sell products that enable or further harm, we can recognize that we face a clear ethical decision. We have an opportunity to transform relationships with others, and probably brighten a corner of our own conscience.

The Growth Choice at Work

We do sometimes have no creative ethical choice at work. We face black-and-white issues where the alternatives are straightforward. But more often than we think, we can exercise courage to choose the pathway that stretches our capacity for personal and interpersonal growth. We can transform the situation for higher-level and longer-term rewards.

Consider the example of Matthew Farmer, formerly an attorney with the 1,200-lawyer firm of Holland & Knight. Farmer, whose story first appeared in the *Wall Street Journal* in 2006, was examining billing records in 2004, when he noticed an alarming discrepancy: an invoice stated he had billed 6.5 hours on the first day of a case for Midwest home builder Pinnacle Corporation.[12] It was a day he recalled clearly, for he had spent just fifteen minutes on the phone in a briefing.

Farmer wondered whether there was a mistake. He checked further and found more than sixty errors in multiple invoices, which together inflated Pinnacle's bill by at least $100,000. When he queried the partner in charge, he was told the time was consistent with the value of the time worked. Farmer disagreed, and he appealed to other lawyers in the firm.

That he even raised the issue makes Farmer an unusual study in the legal profession. A survey released in 2007 showed that roughly two-thirds of lawyers know of bill padding, and most say nothing about it.[13] Farmer would have raised nary an eyebrow had he compromised ethically by saying nothing. He could have avoided lots of embarrassment. He could have avoided a showdown with the senior partner whose reputation he threatened to tarnish. He would even have saved his job.

What did he do? He quit the firm.

Like others in similar straits, Farmer showed we each have a choice. If the ethical environment conflicts with our beliefs, we can avoid the situation by simply going elsewhere. Farmer could have deferred to the elder partner's judgment. Or downplayed the incident and swept it under the rug. But he chose a simple approach: take another job. When opinions on ethics clash, going elsewhere gives us more energy to live a better life, rather than exhaust ourselves swimming upstream in an unhealthy environment. Perhaps in the process Farmer instigated transformation at his old law firm, waking others to the seriousness of their overbilling.

Temptations put us on a balance point between the right thing and the wrong thing. We can stand upright and walk the line of rectitude. We can fall backward into the arms of self-interest and compromise. We can, like Farmer, simply walk away from ethically questionable situations. Or we can step forward to craft transformative solutions for more fulfilling lives.

Charity chief Charles Anderson stepped forward by choosing transparency over the temptation to manage the facts. Taxi driver Osman Chowdhury stepped forward not just by refraining from theft but by going to the trouble to restore lost goods. The frozen-vegetable company's CEO stepped forward by halting deception and instituting a new culture of quality.

These individuals illustrate how we can make a habit of using ethics as a lever. They saw opportunity in taking the high road where others handicap themselves by taking the low road. All of us yearn to act as they did. Some of us have already trained ourselves to do so. The rest of us can start learning to think and act more skillfully today. We can all learn to live a more meaningful life in the face of temptation.

➤ Your Turn: Transform Daily Work

Choose a decision from work that fell into the gray area of ethics. Now use the three skills highlighted in this chapter to rethink how you could have acted had you been more skillful: Clarify the whole truth. Frame the situation as one of relationships. Ask how you would have treated a loved one. What alternatives could/should you have considered to transform relationships at work?

Habit of Wisdom

The Reward of Skillful Ethical Decision Making

Sow a thought, reap an act.
Sow an act, reap a habit.
Sow a habit, reap a character.
Sow a character, reap a destiny.

—Anonymous

S UPPOSE WE LEARNED that when we die we live our current life over, and then live it over again, and so on forever. We do not remember previous lives, so we cannot learn from them. If this were the truth of existence, would it transform us or crush us?

Friedrich Nietzsche, a philosopher who explored this predicament, wrote, "What if some day or night a demon were to . . . say to you: 'This life as you now live it and have lived it you will have to live once again and innumerable times again; and there will be nothing new in it, but every pain and every joy and every thought and sigh and everything unspeakably small or great in your life must return to you . . . The eternal hourglass of existence is turned over again and again, and you with it.'"[1]

If faced with this future, would you exclaim, "Oh boy!" or "Oh shit!"? The answer says a lot about how we have lived.

It also begs the question, What would it take to better our chances of saying, "Oh boy!"? As the authors of this book, we believe one of the things necessary is improving our skillfulness in ethical decision making, enabling us to replace painful ethical compromises with gratifying episodes of character- and relationship-building.

But learning the skills of ethical decision making will not be enough to accomplish such goals. What is also necessary is turning new skills into habits. Only when skills become second nature—our true nature—will we reap a destiny that would make us want to turn that eternal hourglass over again and again.

In ethics as in everything else, developing habits requires repetition and reinforcement. As the saying goes, practice makes perfect—or more accurately, perfect practice makes perfect. That is the final message of this book. If we are to make the most of skillful ethical decision making, we must turn it into a habit.

Research shows that it takes three to four weeks of daily repetition to create a habit. To perform at a high level of competence, it takes even more. Top-rated violinists, for example, have practiced more than ten thousand hours by the time they are twenty. The next tier of experts have practiced seventy-five hundred hours, and the lowest expert tier, five thousand hours.[2] The more practice the better, whether in music or ethics.

If we succeed in turning ethical skillfulness into habits akin to those of musical virtuosos, we wouldn't spend time wringing our hands over how to do the right thing. Johannes Brahms, interviewed late in life, said about composing, "Straightaway, the ideas flow in upon me, directly from God, and not only do I see distinct themes in my mind's eye, but they are clothed in the right forms, harmonies and orchestration. Measure by measure, the finished product is revealed to me."[3]

At the level of Brahms, we don't struggle to solve issues, we transcend them. Like the great moral leaders—Jesus, Buddha, Muhammad, Mother Teresa, Gandhi—we don't have to pause to refer to an ethical code about deceiving, stealing, or harming—any more than we would stop to think about whether to cut off our arms. We have reached a level of understanding about ourselves and the world in which we cease to be tempted. We just do the right thing.

Of course, few of us expect the ethical mastery of either virtuosos or the spiritually enlightened. But with practice we can move in a direction in which we achieve a better sense of the mastery they enjoyed. The farther along this path we get, the less we need to refer to our codes, or exercise the rules of decision analysis. As our ethical sensitivities improve, and as we begin to follow our codes as a matter of habit, we cease conscious decision making altogether.

Our journey starts with practicing the skills in this book. The skill of self-examination. The skill of taking right action according to an ethical code. The skill of using ethical decision-making processes. The skill of seeing temptation as an opportunity for growth, and transforming the temptation into a chance for better living.

What skills should we be developing today? What habits will allow us to respond to Nietzsche's question with increasing confidence, to say we would like to live our lives over?

We cannot do better than making a habit of reflecting regularly on that ancient religious maxim: love your neighbor as yourself. And we cannot reach higher than by interpreting *neighbor* in its broadest sense, to include everyone in our ethical space, not just family and friends but the larger community of humankind.

As Einstein said, "A human being is a part of a whole, called [the] universe, a part limited in time and space. He experiences himself, his thoughts and feelings as something separated from the rest . . . a kind of optical delusion of his consciousness. This delusion is a kind of prison for us, restricting us to our personal desires and to affection for a few persons nearest to us. Our task must be to free ourselves from this prison by widening our circle of compassion to embrace all living creatures and the whole of nature in its beauty."[4]

We can take inspiration from Einstein and other spiritual leaders to guide us in the right direction. The changes will yield worthwhile practical benefits all along the way. We will be able to see ethically awkward situations from afar and avoid them. We will be able to make smart choices about the organizations we join. And when confronted with temptations, we will more often be able to transform them into opportunities for character-and relationship-building.

Instead of finding "good reasons" to compromise, we will find convincing reasons to take right action. Instead of shaving off pieces of our character with faulty thinking, we will think through our decisions skillfully and live more satisfying lives. When we reach the end of our lives, we will carry that much less burden, feel that much less remorse, and create that much more satisfaction from using ethics to make our lives better. Perhaps we will even be inclined to let that hourglass turn upside down.

The Elements of Ethical Thinking

How the Decision Flows

FOR A GRAPHICAL SUMMARY of the key distinctions enabling skillful ethical thinking, see figure A-1. Note how the
distinctions work together. Do not use the figure to guide individual decisions. Instead, use it to guide the flow of your logic, depending on a
decision's characteristics. These distinctions, unique to ethical reasoning,
appear over and over in this book.

The figure hints at the consequences of confusing the dimensions of a
decision. Consider the common mistake, mentioned in chapter 2, of putting prudential actions in the ethical bucket. If we do so, we mistakenly go
through a long decision-making process (top to bottom on the chart) instead of a short one (left to right).

FIGURE A-1

The critical elements of ethical thinking

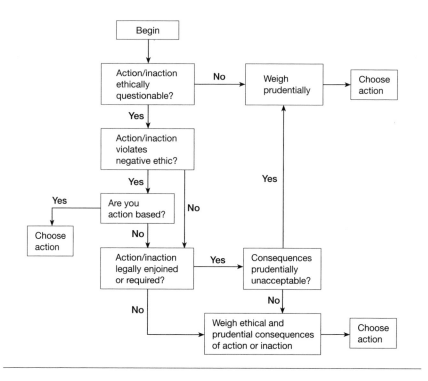

Ethical Codes

Three Examples

O N THE FOLLOWING PAGES are the texts of three ethical codes written by three students who followed the advice in this book. The students produced these codes as a part of either Ron Howard's course at Stanford University or Clint Korver's course at Grinnell College. We have changed the students' names to protect their privacy, and we have edited the codes lightly to make them suitable for publication.

These are not "model" or "textbook" codes. They are long and not always eloquent. But publishing the "perfect" code would give a misleading idea about the way codes turn out in real life. What's important is that the codes allow each person to address personally important issues at a particular moment in their life. The codes represent a journey of personal reflection, a journey necessary for skillful ethical decision making.

For a helpful exercise (suggested at the end of chapter 4), review and annotate these codes to show where they clearly follow or diverge from the advice in this book. Then turn back to your own code, and with the benefit of this added reflection, refine your code.

Megan Gerber—Ethical Code

Ideologically, I am uncomfortable with utilitarianism and consequence-based ethics as underlying frameworks for evaluating truth. In my view, rational implementation of these perspectives requires perfect information—in reality, an unrealistic and rare condition—and the ability to make trade-offs between different considerations (like life, trust, and liberty). I do not feel equipped to make these decisions.

Logically, this would indicate that my entire code should find basis in action-based ethics. Unfortunately, not every part of my life, personality, or reality is entirely logical. While I have used action-based ethics as a guideline for the content herein, I have not yet discerned how to eliminate consequences entirely from ethical considerations. In these sections, my challenge was to reconcile these competing interests in order to create a model that is real for now. As I continue to test these tenets against time and experience, I will continue refining the guidelines and examples below.

Lying

I will strive always to be honest, straightforward, and frank with those around me.

I will strive to communicate with others in a way that enables and empowers them to make informed decisions.

> I will work to detect biases in my own mind-set in order to improve the completeness of truths I relay to others.

> I will respect the rights of other people to form their own opinions and decisions based on facts they gather from me or from other sources. I will not manipulate these outcomes.

I will strive to tell complete truths when situations are immediately relevant to those around me.

> I will not deliberately withhold relevant information from a person when it is immediately relevant to her.

> In situations where the circumstances are not time-sensitive, I may wait to reveal additional information until a time when it is immediately pertinent.

I will not withhold part of the truth in order to personally profit from another's ignorance.

In no case will I allow the behavior of others to affect my will to tell the truth.

If others abuse my honesty, I will decrease my trust in proportion to the violation.

I will not lie to anyone based on past breaches of my trust. In adjusting my forthrightness, I will withhold entire truths, not mere parts. This will allow me to use caution when divulging information while still striving to communicate all sides of relevant issues.

I will not make promises I do not intend to keep or am not capable of keeping.

If conditions change and I am no longer able to keep a promise I have made, I will be proactive in notifying other parties to the promise of what they can truly expect.

I will act as expediently as possible in these situations, regardless of the promise's relative importance to other priorities in my life. Promises by nature are an automatic priority due to their seriousness in maintaining a level of trust.

I will maintain confidentiality when I have committed to doing so, except in situations where keeping information secret jeopardizes the life or safety of another person.

I will not promise confidentiality in situations where I know the law requires me to divulge information.

For example, when working with children, I will not make blind commitments to keep secrets, as I may be legally required to report child abuse.

I will strive to notify others of my life-and-safety exceptions to confidentiality prior to their divulging information to me.

I will exercise caution when engaging in games of partial truth.

I will not lie in debate.

I will not utilize games of partial truth to deliberately create doubt or suspicion about real-world truths. (I will avoid making comments or taking action that blurs the lines between the game and reality. For example, in artistic expression, I will not tell lies that may change the way people think about the world or each other.)

I will not knowingly profit from the ignorance of others.

I will not cheat on exams, other coursework, or their equivalents in my professional life.

I will not ask for extensions or exceptions in cases where, knowing the full truth, I would not grant them for myself. I will be complete and honest in explaining situations in which I fail to follow through with assignments or similar commitments.

I will not lie about reasons for missing class or turning assignments in late.

I will not tell white lies, or lies involving "trivial, diplomatic, or well-intentioned mistruths." (As defined in Wikipedia.)

I will view these temptations as opportunities to deepen my relationships with others by telling the truth.

I will strive to use language that is accurate, precise, and appropriate. I will avoid intentionally misleading through rhetoric, whether or not my statements are technically true.

I will strive to remain alert and cognizant in situations where I may be tempted to exaggerate in any form. I will avoid knowingly distorting the magnitude of any truth, mistruth, or event.

I will avoid euphemism, cacophemism, hyperbole, and other linguistic magnifiers whenever possible.

In situations where I am not capable of discerning the truth, I will strive to present all sides of the story without bias.

When statistics can support multiple results, I will be forthright in presenting the multiple conclusions possible.

Harming

I will not initiate harm or physical violence toward others.

> In a dire case of self-defense, I will use no more force than
> absolutely necessary to escape the situation.

I will alert authorities of physical altercations rather than becoming
involved myself.

I will not drink and drive, park in fire lanes, or operate motor vehicles
unless I am completely alert, aware of my surroundings, and well-equipped
to drive.

Only in the case that a loved one in pain has created a living will indi-
cating interest and intent will I consider assisting in suicide. While these
conditions are necessary, they are not wholly sufficient.

I will not use physical tools of war or destruction to commit any violent act except in cases where it is absolutely critical for escaping a direct
attacker as specified above.

Stealing

I will not steal items in cases where effects on other individuals are clear.
This includes items from stores, shops, or other physical establishments. I
hope that with time this tenet can be reduced to "I will not steal."

> I will not take advantage of generosity or autonomy offered by my
> employer.

> I will not embezzle.

> I will not take advantage of trust or ignorance of customers or
> others, either for my benefit or for that of my employer.

> I will make attempts when possible to return items for which I was
> not charged, or for which I was charged incorrectly. I will make at
> least as much effort to correct errors that benefit me as I would to
> correct errors that disadvantage me.

> I will strive in every case to give credit to others where credit is
> due. I will not plagiarize or exploit the intellectual property of
> others in my own work.

I will allocate at least as much energy in returning a lost item I have found as the item itself is worth. Whenever possible, I will turn lost items over to relevant authorities.

Special Treatment

I will strive to treat *everyone* as I wish to be treated.

I will be glad to enhance opportunity for my loved ones through normal means, but will not use my influence or other relationships to advantage them over other applicants.

I will abstain from influencing hiring processes in which my friends or loved ones are competing. (In cases where applications are blind, I will withdraw from the decision-making process the moment I have reasonable suspicion of a conflict of interest.)

I will be honest and complete in all recommendation letters and interviews, regardless of personal relationships.

Business Ethics

I will not allow employer incentives to influence or bend my ethical code, nor will I accept jobs whose requirements violate this code.

I will not steal or embezzle from my employer, nor will I steal or embezzle on behalf of my employer.

I will not conceal or assist in concealing illegal behavior (mine or others') in the workplace.

I will not create incentives for others to act unethically.

Proximity to Unethical Behavior

I firmly believe that if all of the world's "good people" worked only for the world's "good companies," few faulty, unethical, or atrocious processes would ever be reformed. Therefore, while I will not forbid myself from working for operations whose underlying premises I do not share, I will remain alert when near unethical behavior and will strive to avoid dulling my instinctual sensitivities at all costs. While I may accept a job for a company with the intent to change its practices, I am not willing to violate any tenet of my ethical code in the process. I will strive always to abide by my personal ethical code, regardless of others' actions.

While I may take a job as a financial operative in a cigarette company, I will avoid directly contributing to marketing practices I find to be unethical.

I will not accept work when job requirements and expectations violate my ethical code. This includes frontline work with the armed forces and police departments.

I will strive to respect ethical sensitivities and trust my instincts when entering proximity to unethical behavior.

I will work to avoid situations of ethical sensitivity where I cannot discern a workable means for personally influencing change and improvement.

I will work to keep a fresh perspective in companies where questionable practices occur, and will speak out in favor of reform wherever possible and appropriate.

Reproductive Issues

I will seek and obtain active consent before engaging in any romantic activities.

I will not engage in romantic activities in cases where I am not entirely comfortable dealing with the "worst-case" outcome.

I will not provoke the possibility of pregnancy unless absolutely certain that my partner and I are capable and likely to make cooperative, mature, and level-headed decisions about how to deal with an accidental conception.

I will take precautions against sexually transmitted diseases.

I will maintain honest, openly communicative relationships with all romantic partners.

I will inform all of my relevant partners of issues involving sexually transmitted diseases, pregnancy, or their general health as proactively and early as possible.

I will respect the final decision-making authority of my loved ones in making decisions about their own bodies. While I will express my opinion freely in discussion and debate, I will strive to accept and support their ultimate choices.

I will not engage in romantic activities with individuals who are in committed relationships with others. I will ask about commitments before deciding to become involved. If I discover that a commitment does exist, contrary to what I have been told, I will discontinue my involvement immediately.

I will utilize great discretion when engaging in romantic activities with the former partners of my friends, colleagues, or acquaintances. I will not engage in these activities with individuals who may still be dating my friends, or for whom my friends still have feelings.

I will attempt to be understanding and liberal if my friends end up in relationships with my ex-boyfriends after a reasonable grace period has passed.

Abortion

I will not consider abortion past a point when a fetus could survive on its own.

I will consult my partner and will respect his input in making an ultimate decision regarding abortion.

Raphael Copters—Ethical Code

The ethical code follows, organized by major categories with analyses directly following rules.

Truth Telling

I. DECEPTION. I will lie if it will not harm the person lied to/about and the total gain (excluding my own) is greater than the damage done. The damage done must be able to be explained to the people being lied to upon the conclusion of the incident.

II. SECRETS. I will keep the confidentiality of friends, family, and colleagues as long as there are no long-term negative consequences by keeping their secrets.

Example: I see my friend's girlfriend outside a restaurant kissing another man. I decide to tell my friend what I saw because I know how he feels about honesty in a relationship. His girlfriend could continue this behavior without ever letting my friend know and end up putting a long-term strain on their relationship.

III. PROMISES. I will keep promises I make to others and expect others to keep theirs as long as no unforeseeable events occur that end up taking priority or prevent me from keeping the promise.

Example: I promise to be my friend's best man, but then my mother falls seriously ill and is hospitalized. Even though both situations are once-in-a-lifetime events (and are thus equal in that sense), I would choose to break my promise to my friend, and visit and take care of my mother because, as family, she holds higher priority than does my friend.

IV. CHEATING. I will not cheat or condone others' cheating. When faced with an unfair situation where others are cheating, I will not stoop to their level by also cheating.

Example: I play poker in Las Vegas and see two players that are collaborating with each other underneath the table. Instead of stooping to their level and ganging up on them with my other friend at the table, I choose to walk away and simply avoid playing with them in the future. Even though I have already been cheated, I will not "return the favor" in order to recoup my losses. It should be noted that in an honor code situation, where it is also part of the responsibility of the student to enforce the code, I will take the necessary steps in order to ensure that the honor code is upheld, despite the fact that, in this example, I would not have for prudential reasons.

Killing/Harming

I will harm directly only if I am being harmed and not before, even if I know I will be harmed: in this case, I will do all I can to avoid the situation.

V. ANIMAL RIGHTS. I will not kill animals for sport if I deem it is wasteful killing.

Frivolous or recreational hunting is not something I would engage in because there is no purpose to the killing. The recreational value of the activity will have no value to me in an ethical decision; if it is not wasteful (for example, catching one fish, then eating it), then I am willing to participate.

I would conduct animal testing if the objective of the experiments would serve the greater good of society.

I would approve of animal testing for medical solutions and benefits, such as a cure for diseases and cancer, but not for consumer products that do not physically improve the quality of life (such as perfume).

VI. IMPOSING RISK. I will not unnecessarily impose risk on others unless I deem that the benefit of my actions is so much greater than the risk on them that it becomes negligible.

"So much greater" in the above rule is likely the vaguest phrase used in this ethical code: as a result, I limit it to mean only the most trivial of risks. For instance, I will force a friend to take the risk of going outside without an umbrella despite a high risk of rain if I view that there is another situation that requires his immediate attention. Such a risk carries no significant consequences, and therefore I will have no long-term qualms about imposing this risk on him.

VII. ASSISTED SUICIDE. I will not assist in another's suicide—I have no right to make such a decision about another's life. I will, however, accept another's decision to kill himself by the same reasoning—I have no right to make a decision about his life.

Reproductive Issues

VIII. ABORTION. I condone legal abortions because I personally do not feel it is taking a life away as long as it is within the first two trimesters. However, because abortion is inevitably a decision made between both my partner and me, I am willing to concede the decision to my partner if I judge that her opinion on the matter is stronger than mine.

My opinions on the matter are not particularly strong, and as a result, I will respect my partner's decision in this regard as long as the following conditions for guardianship are also met.

IX. GUARDIANSHIP. I will not adopt for prudential issues, but I will condone others' adoptions if I judge that they can financially afford to take care of a child long-term and be personally vested in his or her interests.

Professional Ethics

X. EXPLOITATION OF A PROFESSIONAL SITUATION FOR PER-
SONAL GAIN. I will not use any knowledge gained from my position
for personal gains, even if there are no immediately apparent victims of
such a decision.

Regardless of the fact that I may not immediately perceive any ill effects to others, use of this information may eventually lead to ill effects
unbeknownst to me as a result of an unfair advantage that I exploited.

XI. I will not work for a company whose products will likely be used
in a manner that will conflict with my ethical values.

For instance, I will not work for piracy groups that aim to crack software to distribute pirated software or media available for download. Although the cracking of the software itself is not necessarily harmful (for
instance, in projects requiring the resetting of configurations of certain
equipment or programs), the act of doing so for a piracy group is likely to
lead to malicious use of the product.

XII. Awareness of a company's ethics is required before working for
them; ignorance of its ethics is wrong because it will potentially lead to
many ethically sensitive situations I should aim to minimize.

XIII. If I accept a job without understanding the ethical consequences of doing so, then the ethically sensitive situations arising from
that job can only be attributed to myself.

Special Treatment Category

XIV. NEPOTISM. I would help family and friends as long as it is not
taking away someone else's opportunity and they are capable of or will
become capable of doing the job (even if not immediately qualified to do so).

In this case, I have a positive ethic to help my family and friends attain
the best opportunities available to them. This, however, is trumped by the
more important negative ethic of preventing people from unfairly attaining
positions that would have otherwise been open to others who are more
qualified.

XV. AFFIRMATIVE ACTION. Affirmative action, under my view, is a subset of nepotism as a favored response to a certain party for a limited opportunity. As a result, if it takes away a "spot" from an otherwise more qualified person, then I will not support it and will view it as ethically wrong and of a magnitude equal to favoring an unqualified friend over a qualified job seeker.

XVI. BRIBES. I will not bribe when I am giving incentive for a person to do an action that is against his or her moral inclinations or would negatively impact someone else's opportunity.

For instance, if I tip a hotel concierge $20 for a nicer room because it is my honeymoon, so long as that room was not reserved for someone else already, I do not consider that bribing. However, I would not give $20 to a host or hostess to avoid a long wait for tables at a restaurant, because I would be gaining at the expense of everyone else who was waiting before me.

It should be noted that my analysis is of a largely recreational situation, the one most likely to occur in regular life (when the line is difficult to draw between bribing and tipping). If it becomes a legal situation (and expectation), then my views are likely to change.

In this situation, if the expectation is to bribe, then I will bribe—if it is expected, it no longer has the same implication of a regular bribe, which is to cause an otherwise unwarranted benefit for this payment. When it is expected, that bribe brings an expected, rather than unwarranted, benefit.

Stealing

XVII. I will steal only if it is a necessity for survival and the item is not a necessity to the person who owns it. The item must ultimately be compensated for or returned.

1. Stealing would only occur in extreme circumstances, where I did not have the financial means or the appropriate time for proper protocol to follow. Below is an example of stealing due to financial reasons.
   a. If my child were severely sick and needed medicine in order to survive that I could not afford, I would steal it from the pharmacy given the conditions that (1) there are multiple in stock, hence I am not taking away a necessity of a single

supply and (2) I will pay back the value of its worth once I earn back the money, making sure rightful compensation is given when I can afford it.

2. Below is a variation of the above example of stealing when there is not enough time for normal procedure.
   a. I am switching between medical insurance companies. Due to my son's illness, I cannot wait for the insurance companies to sort out the discrepancies, and I cannot afford to pay for the medicine without the proper co-pay. Thus, I would steal due to the timeliness of the issue instead of waiting for proper protocol.

XVIII. I will not steal anything that is rightfully owned by someone else, unless I am taking it away to avoid harmful effects.

For example, if a friend of mine is recovering from lung cancer and wants to keep smoking, I will steal his cigarettes to prevent him from smoking and subjecting himself to a worse medical condition.

Proximity to Unethical Behavior

XIX. Depending on how close or personally vested I am in the situation, I would take actions if I witnessed unethical behavior.

For instance, I do not have personal relationships or ties regarding the Israeli-Palestinian conflict, so even though my tax dollars are supporting the Israeli side, I do not feel the need to protest, because the situation is too removed from my interests.

XX. If I see someone shoplifting minor items from a store, such as a loaf of bread, I will not run to stop them from continuing to do so. I will not judge their decision and their reasons (unknown to me) to do so, and I will not report something of relatively small value for the store.

However, if I happen to see during a final exam two people cheating by comparing answers with each other in the middle of the test, I will feel obligated and personally invested to report this behavior because of (1) the honor code, where part of my responsibility is to enforce it, and (2) the unfairness for myself and the other students because we are graded on a curve basis, so that the unfair advantage the two cheaters are getting will negatively impact the rest of the class who are following the honor code.

Deepti Chandna—Ethical Code

Personal Ethics

1. TRUTH TELLING

a. I will not lie or present the truth in a deceptive manner unless:

- My lying sòmehow saves someone's life (could be mine, a loved one's, or a stranger's).

- My lying somehow prevents physical harm from being inflicted on anyone.

b. I will keep a secret if I promise to do so, unless by revealing it I save somebody's life or prevent them from physical harm. (This judgment shall be made by me, with the best possible information I can get.)

c. If I make a promise, I shall keep it. I shall consider all verbal promises like contracts and abide by them.

d. I shall not cheat in any setting (academic or business).

e. While communicating the truth to someone, I shall use language that is simple and value neutral, to convey the whole truth. (Positive ethic.)

f. If I know that someone is communicating a falsehood, I shall confront them about it.

g. If I know that someone is cheating, I will confront them about it. (Includes academic, business, or infidelity.)

2. KILLING, HARMING, PREVENTING HARM

- I shall not kill anybody, unless it is in self-defense or in defense of a loved one.

- I shall kill if somebody threatens the use of force with intent to kill, even if they haven't made the first move yet.

- I shall not drive under the influence of alcohol. If I feel even slightly light-headed, I shall get a ride or shall wait until the light-headedness passes before I get behind the wheel.

- I shall not eat animals.

- I shall only buy "free farm" milk when the option is available, even if it is more expensive to do so. I believe treatment of dairy animals is an ethically sensitive issue, and what we pay for is a message of what we believe is important.

- I shall not assist in suicide; however, I will not use force to prevent someone from committing suicide if they have thoroughly thought it through and are entirely sure they want to do it, however much this decision may cause pain to me.

- I shall stop bullies who are bullying someone, even if I don't know them.

- I shall stop anyone who stones a dog on the road. I shall use force against them to do so, if required.

- I shall never conduct research that requires the killing of multicellular organisms that are not fungi, coelenterates, porifera (sponges). That is, I shall not conduct research that requires the killing of animals that are of the rank platyhelminths and above (as per animal classification followed by biologists in 2006).

3. STEALING

- I shall not steal unless it is to protect someone's life.[1]

- I do not consider piracy a theft from an ethical point of view. I do not think downloading music from the Internet or buying cheap books is "stealing."[2]

- I would not steal to make life more easy or comfortable.

Reproductive Issues

In this section I have even listed those issues that I believe are not ethically sensitive to clarify my views on them. Even though this is an ethical code, I think it is important to note those issues that may be commonly seen in many others' ethical codes, and indicate that I believe they are ethically neutral topics, just so it is known that I have thought of them.

- I do not believe stem cell research is unethical. I would use the benefits of such research, or fund such research, or work for a company that does such research.

- I believe that sperm and egg donation are not ethically sensitive issues; I feel it's an entirely prudential matter.

- I believe surrogate motherhood is not an ethically sensitive issue. It's a prudential and legal matter only.

Professional Ethics

1. TYPE OF WORK

- I will not join an organization whose goals are antithetical to my ethics. Thus I will not work for a company that makes weapons.[3]

- For companies whose goals cause them to behave unethically (and this is not an intrinsic part of the goal itself—in the first point, it would be war), I will work for them only in the following cases: either I work directly in fixing the issue,[4] or if the company is used to behaving unethically, my being a part of the organization will help it stop doing that.[5]

2. MISREPRESENTATION OF DATA

- I will not misreport or misrepresent data to support or oppose any person's point of view (even if my boss asked me to). I will present the facts in such a way as to endeavor to tell the truth, and the whole truth, to the best of my professional judgment.

- If I am aware of misrepresentation of facts or data, I will speak up and address my concerns to my superiors. In short, I will not let things hang vaguely in the air. I will call a spade a spade if someone is calling it a diamond. I will do this in as prudential and intelligent a way as possible.

- If data and/or conclusions drawn from gathered data are unclear, I will state the uncertainty of my conclusions or data along with the presentation of the data, even if my reservations don't support my point.

3. OFFICE SUPPLIES

- I do not consider usage of office supplies to be an ethical issue when working with for-profit corporations, but I have put it in my code to clarify this point.

- When working for a nonprofit organization, I shall check the general policy regarding office supplies before using them.

4. TIME AT WORK

- I shall never misreport hours worked.

- I shall work at the job the company is paying me to do for all of the time I clock as hours worked.

- I shall not make personal phone calls, check personal e-mail, or read personal items on the Internet on company time. If the company says it is all right to do so, then I will allocate a part of my break to this purpose.

- I do not consider drinking coffee, tea, juice, water, or other company-provided refreshments to be ethically sensitive. I shall not hoard treats and give them to other people, but shall not be economic in consuming them myself.

Miscellaneous

1. BRIBERY

- I shall not bribe someone, unless it is to save someone's life.

- I shall not accept a bribe ever.

2. FAVORITISM/NEPOTISM/RACISM

- I shall not consider somebody's gender, race, or caste when hiring them for a job. If two people are equally suited for a position, the odds of either one getting the position should be one-half.

Notes:

1. This is a hypothetical situation. Suppose someone were dying, and I didn't have money to buy them food or medicines or medical care. Suppose that even after asking for it, I weren't able to procure the required supplies. Then I would steal for it.

2. I know of many roadside book markets that print and publish books without paying copyright to the publisher. I have heard many authors say they are happy if more people read their work, and I agree. I think the success of a book lies not in how much money it generates but in how many people read it. I also don't believe we're depriving anyone else of the book (and thus it is different from stealing a book from a store).

3. Any company whose products are successful and used only in case of war. A company making fighter planes would thus also fall in this category. Or a company making nuclear bombs. (Note that this does not include a company that manufactures aircraft for civilian purposes, nor does it include a nuclear power plant, which are peaceful uses of the same technology.) If a company has both departments (for instance, if the same company uses technology for both peaceful and warring purposes), then I would be wary of joining it and would join it only if I did not have an offer from a company that is entirely peaceful.

4. A company that has violated a contract and is trying to unethically get around the issue (e.g., breach of an environmental permit). I will work with them to make them ethical in their processes— clean them up from the inside, so to speak.

5. The government, World Health Organization, United Nations, The World Bank.

Ethics for the Real World presents a variety of new and unique messages. To make them easy to find and remember, we list them below in the order they appear in the book. Use this list to refresh your memory or locate page numbers for relevant passages and key examples.

Introduction: Skillful Decision Making

(*Example:* the defense contractor solicits a bogus analysis)

Chapter 1: Almost Ethical

Chapter 2: Draw Distinctions

Chapter 3: Consult the Touchstones

Chapter 4: Draft Your Code

Chapter 5: Choose Action

Chapter 6: Transform Life

Chapter 7: Transform Work

Epilogue: Habit of Wisdom

ACKNOWLEDGMENTS

We would like to thank our many great students over the last few decades. In particular, we would like to thank those who gave us permission to use their personal examples in this book: Omar A. Al-Saif, Mike Boutross, Deepti Chatti, Megan Goering, David Huynh, Jessie Juusola, Boyi Low, Junayd Mahmood, Somik Raha, Cliff Redeker, Chester Shiu, Will Tang, Jonathan Yi-Kwang Teo, and Neal Vora.

We would also like to thank Bill Birchard, our writer. Bill did an excellent job helping us to convert material optimized for a Socratic approach to teaching ethics to graduate students to a form accessible to a much broader audience. He also managed our project with a skilled and firm hand. With his help, we kept to a schedule and delivered a completed manuscript on time.

We would like to thank our agent, Helen Rees, who helped us find a home for the book. Our editor at Harvard Business Press, Jacque Murphy, then pushed us to make the book better, and we appreciate her comments and insight.

There have been many others who have meaningfully contributed to this project, including Charles Anderson, CEO, United Way of the National Capital Area; Ibrahim Mojel, Ron's teaching assistant for his ethics class over the last few years; four anonymous reviewers; and the team at Harvard Business Press.

We would like to separately thank people important to each of our efforts.

Ron Howard

The foundations of this book go back thirty years, to a time when I realized my work on improving human decisions was essentially amoral. When and whether to use tools like a computer, for example, would often have ethical implications. It was my responsibility to provide students with a means of increasing their ethical sensitivity. The graduate course that resulted has benefited from many contributions from many others, not only from students, but also from the dozens of teaching assistants who have continually improved the quality of the experience. I thank them all.

While I had often thought of writing this book, I thank Clint Korver for the energy and enthusiasm that made it possible: Clint's contributions appear in every aspect of content and form. If "a teacher is known by his students," I could not be better known.

Clint Korver

I would like to thank my wife, Miriam Rivera, for her insights into how to Tell the Whole Truth in more useful ways. Miriam contributed to this book in many big and small ways. More important, I would like to thank her for helping me live a life consistent with my ethical code. I would also like to thank my two daughters, Serena Rivera-Korver and Sophia Rivera-Korver, for the happy faces and whiteboard love notes that made the evening and weekend work on this book more pleasurable. I would also like to thank my parents and sister for creating an ethical touchstone that has served me well throughout my life.

Finally, I would like to thank my friend, coauthor, and teacher, Ron Howard. In addition to teaching me the tools of my profession, Ron has provided an example of how to live a meaningful life.

Introduction

1. *Saint Thomas Aquinas quote*: See Saint Thomas Aquinas, *Summa Theologica, prima secundæ partis*, question 95, article 1.

2. *Zogby international poll*: The Zogby poll, "U.S. Public Widely Distrusts Its Leaders," was released on May 23, 2006. As of this writing, it was available at http://www.zogby.com/search/ReadNews.dbm?ID=1116.

3. *Research by Philip Zimbardo*: Zimbardo has conducted and gathered a fascinating collection of research showing how situations induce average people to do evil deeds. Situations, says Zimbardo, have a way of knocking out thinking processes, suspending "conscience, self-awareness, sense of personal responsibility, obligation, commitment, liability, morality and analyses in terms of costs/benefits of given actions." See Philip G. Zimbardo, "A Situationist Perspective on the Psychology of Evil: Understanding How Good People Are Transformed into Perpetrators," in *The Social Psychology of Good and Evil: Understanding Our Capacity for Kindness and Cruelty*, ed. Arthur G. Miller (New York: Guilford, 2004), 26.

Chapter 1

1. *Psychiatrists earn headline billing*: As in many cases of conflicts of interest, the cause is probably ethical insensitivity and a lack of awareness, not mal-intent. In a world with an ever-increasing emphasis on transparency, the number of transgressions is all the more notable. In its front-page box, the *Journal* singled out Lori Altshuler, Vivien K. Burt, Lee S. Cohen, and Adele C. Viguera for unreported financial links to drugmakers. See David Armstrong, "Side Effects: Financial Ties to Drug Makers Cloud Major Depression Study," *Wall Street Journal*, July 11, 2006.

2. *They didn't disclose that they moonlighted*: In the original article, most authors disclosed no conflicts at all, when in fact dozens of disclosures were required by *JAMA* policy. See Lee S. Cohen, Lori Altshuler, Bernard L. Harlow, Ruta Nonacs, Jeffrey Newport, Adele C. Viguera, Rita Suri, Vivien K. Burt, Victoria Hendrick, Alison M. Reminick, Ada Loughead, Allison F. Vitonis, and Zachary N. Stowe, "Relapse of Major Depression During Pregnancy in Women Who Maintain or Discontinue Antidepressant Treatment—Correction," *Journal of the American Medical Association* 296, no. 2 (2006): 499–507. In the correction now attached to the article, the passage on Altshuler, for example, is as follows:

"Dr Altshuler is a consultant to Abbott Laboratories, Eli Lilly, Forest Pharmaceuticals, Janssen Pharmaceutica, Pfizer, Solvay, and Bristol-Myers Squibb; receives grant support from Abbott, Eli Lilly, Forest, GlaxoSmithKline, and Solvay; has received honoraria from Abbott, Bristol-Myers Squibb, Eli Lilly, Forest, and GlaxoSmithKline; and is on the speakers bureaus and/or advisory boards of Abbott, AstraZeneca, Bristol-Myers Squibb, Eli Lilly, Forest, GlaxoSmithKline, Pfizer, Wyeth, and Solvay."

3. *Medical publishing has been roiled*: The editor of *JAMA* summarized the journal's long battle to improve conflict-of-interest disclosure, starting in 1985. See Catherine D. DeAngelis, "The Influence of Money on Medical Science," *Journal of the American Medical Association* 296, no. 8 (2006). As recently as 2005, she had drawn attention to disclosure policies, saying, "JAMA requires complete disclosure of all relevant financial relationships and potential financial conflicts of interest, regardless of amount or value." See Phil B. Fontanarosa, Annette Flanagin, and Catherine D. DeAngelis, "Reporting Conflicts of Interest, Financial Aspects of Research, and Role of Sponsors in Funded Studies," *Journal of the American Medical Association* 294, no. 1 (2005): 110–111.

4. *Research shows some defects*: Research continues into birth defects that may be associated with the class of antidepressants known as selective serotonin-reuptake inhibitors (SSRIs). As of this writing, research showed an increase in defects, though minor. For a report on breathing disorders, see Christina D. Chambers et al., "Selective Serotonin-Reuptake Inhibitors and Risk of Persistent Pulmonary Hypertension of the Newborn," *New England Journal of Medicine* 354, no. 6 (2006). More recent research includes two studies: Carol Louik et al., "First-Trimester Use of Selective Serotonin-Reuptake Inhibitors and the Risk of Birth Defects," *New England Journal of Medicine* 356, no. 26 (2007): 2675–2683; and Sura Alwan et al., "Use of Selective Serotonin-Reuptake Inhibitors in Pregnancy and the Risk of Birth Defects," *New England Journal of Medicine* 356, no. 26 (2007): 2684–2692.

5. *Some readers were unhappy*: One of the most vocal was an obstetrician who complained in part, "It is . . . essential that readers be aware that the majority of the authors have been paid by companies that manufacture antidepressants, and that the lead author appears to have received support from at least 8 such companies." See Adam C. Urato, "Letters: Antidepressant Treatment and Relapse of Depression During Pregnancy," *Journal of the American Medical Association* 296, no. 2 (2006): 166.

6. *The authors were tops*: In response to *JAMA*'s request, the authors said they felt their financial links were irrelevant, because their research was not the result of testing individual drugs, the study was federally funded, the patients themselves decided what to do, and the data was analyzed by objective parties. Still, they had repeatedly received money from drugmakers. They expressed regret and offered full disclosure in a subsequent issue of *JAMA*. See Lee S. Cohen, Lori Altshuler, Bernard L. Harlow, Ruta Nonacs, Jeffrey Newport, Adele C. Viguera, Rita Suri, Vivien K. Burt, Victoria Hendrick, Alison M. Reminick, Ada Loughead, Allison F. Vitonis, and Zachary N. Stowe, "Letters: Antidepressant Treatment and Relapse of Depression During Pregnancy," *Journal of the American Medical Association* 296, no. 2 (2006): 166–167.

7. *In one study of lying*: See Bella M. DePaulo et al., "Lying in Everyday Life," *Journal of Personality and Social Psychology* 70, no. 5 (1996): 979–995.

8. *Kenny Rogers's pine tar patch*: Reporter Joshua Prager wrote a thoughtful account of the pitching incident. See Joshua Prager, "In the Fray: Baseball's Dirty Open Secret," *Wall Street Journal*, October 26, 2006.

9. *Studies of thousands of students*: The Center for Academic Integrity posts cheating and plagiarism results online. See http://www.academicintegrity.org/cai_research .asp.

10. *A study of medical residents*: The reports by medical residents give a stark picture of how frequently highly motivated professionals indulge in mistruths. See Michael J. Green et al., "Lying to Each Other: When Internal Medicine Residents Use Deception with Their Colleagues," *Archives of Internal Medicine* 160, no. 15 (2000): 2317–2323.

11. *The professor and his tomatoes*: The professor is Ron Howard, an author of this book, who finds that the small episodes of ethical compromise often illustrate the big mistakes in ethical thinking. The tomato episode occurred in the late 1960s.

12. *Study of lying in romantic relationships*: We may tell ourselves we lie for the benefit of loved ones, but our partners don't see it that way. Tellingly, liars reported feeling guilty about lying even though they said their lies were altruistic. See Mary E. Kaplar and Anne K. Gordon, "The Enigma of Altruistic Lying: Perspective Differences in What Motivates and Justifies Lie Telling Within Romantic Relationships," *Personal Relationships* 11, no. 4 (2004): 489, 497.

13. *President Bill Clinton infamously said*: For a wrap-up of the Monica Lewinsky obfuscation, see Peter Baker and John F. Harris, "Clinton Admits to Lewinsky Relationship, Challenges Starr to End Personal 'Prying,'" *Washington Post*, August 18, 1998.

14. *Abraham Lincoln relied on deception*: Lincoln campaigned against the extension of slavery, not against slavery itself, although he would tell abolitionists slavery was evil. His comments illustrate the contortions of professional politicians looking for votes. See Richard Hofstadter, *The American Political Tradition: And the Men Who Made It* (1948; repr., New York: Vintage Books, 1989), 144, 149, 150.

15. *Scientists admitting to misbehavior*: See Brian C. Martinson, Melissa S. Anderson, and Raymond de Vries, "Scientists Behaving Badly," *Nature* 435 (2005): 737–738.

16. *Case of Merck's Vioxx pain reliever*: The original paper on Vioxx describes extenuating issues leading the researchers to their conclusions. Still, the study design remained questionable, and even after the Food and Drug Administration posted revised data on its Web site in February 2001, Merck continued to market the drug aggressively. For the original study, see Claire Bombardier et al., "Comparison of Upper Gastrointestinal Toxicity of Rofecoxib and Naproxen in Patients with Rheumatoid Arthritis," *New England Journal of Medicine* 343 (2000): 1520–1528. Vioxx was pulled from the market in September 2004. In the aftermath, observers questioned the slow action by the *New England Journal of Medicine*. See David Armstrong, "Bitter Pill: How the New England Journal Missed Warning Signs on Vioxx," *Wall Street Journal*, May 15, 2006. The original study authors continued to insist they followed appropriate clinical trial principles and would not correct their article. For a summary of the dispute, see Wayne Kondro, "Dispute over Vioxx Study Plays Out in New England Journal," *Canadian Medical Association Journal* 174, no. 10 (2006): 1397. The *New England Journal* reaffirmed its censure in Gregory D. Curfman, Stephen Morrissey, and Jeffrey M. Drazen, "Expression of Concern Reaffirmed," *New England Journal of Medicine* 354, no. 11 (2006): 1193.

17. *George Orwell's comments on language*: See George Orwell, *A Collection of Essays* (New York: Harvest Books, 1970), 166, 171.

18. *Hank Greenberg's foot faults*: See Randall Smith, "Greenberg's Pals Ship a Letter Rallying Support," *Wall Street Journal*, October 29, 2005.

19. *William Jefferson taking bribes*. As of this writing, William Jefferson was fighting the charges. For the story of the initial sting, see Dana Milbank, "So $90,000 Was in the Freezer. What's Wrong with That?" *Washington Post*, May 23, 2006.

20. *Harris survey of office pilfering*: "Plants, Décor and Furniture Among the Items Office Workers Admit to Stealing, New Survey Finds," May 1, 2006. As of this writing, the survey was available at http://research.lawyers.com/common/content/print_content.php?articleid=1037764&.

21. *Cable television signal theft*: Rob Stoddard and Brian Dietz, "New Survey Finds Significant Drop in Cable Theft Rate," National Cable & Telecommunications Association, April 11, 2005. As of this writing, the survey was available at http://www.ncta.com/ContentView .aspx?hidenavlink=true&type=reltyp1&contentId=367.

22. *Patrick Schiltz on attorney bill padding*: Schiltz makes a provocative case for the inevitability of bill padding in most big law firms. See Patrick J. Schiltz, "On Being a Happy, Healthy, and Ethical Member of an Unhappy, Unhealthy, and Unethical Profession," *Vanderbilt Law Review* 52 (1999): 917.

23. *Experiments by Stanley Milgram*: Milgram's experiment stands as a perennial reminder of how easily normal people will harm others, even when they know the circumstances are contrived. See Stanley Milgram, "Behavioral Study of Obedience," *Journal of Abnormal and Social Psychology* 67 (1963): 371–378. For the virtual reprise of Milgram's experiment, see M. Slater et al., "A Virtual Reprise of the Stanley Milgram Obedience Experiments," *PLoS ONE* 1, no. 1 (2006). As of this writing, this was online at http:// www.plosone.org/article/fetchArticle.action?articleURI=info%3Adoi%2F10.1371%2Fjournal. pone.0000039.

24. *Legitimization of state-controlled killing*: For our account of state-supported killing of children and the insane, we rely on the work of Robert Jay Lifton. Physicians, as Lifton shows, succumbed to the same kind of thinking as volunteers in the Milgram experiment. Writes Lifton, "The institutional doctor . . . was at the killing edge of the medical structure, whatever the regime's assurance that the state took full responsibility. Yet he developed—in fact, cultivated—the sense that, as an agent of the state, he was powerless." See Robert Jay Lifton, *The Nazi Doctors: Medical Killing and the Psychology of Genocide* (New York: Basic Books, 1986), 46, 50, 51, 56, 71, 106. These atrocities are also covered elsewhere. The figure of ninety thousand murders of the adult insane and the information about combustibility experiments come from Robert Edwin Herzstein, *The Nazis*, World War II Series (Alexandria, VA: Time-Life Books, 1980), 141, 147.

25. *Topf engineers Fritz Sander and Karl Schultze*: The stories of Sander and Schultze come from transcripts of postwar testimony given by each man. See http://www .jewishvirtuallibrary.org/jsource/Holocaust/sander.html and http://www.jewishvirtuallibrary .org/jsource/Holocaust/Schultze.html.

Chapter 2

1. *Albert Camus quote*: Albert Camus, *The Plague* (New York: Modern Library, 1948).

2. *Kurt Gerstein's story*: Gerstein's story has been told in at least two books. We relied principally on the account by Saul Friedländer. The account by Pierre Joffroy includes a translation of one of Gerstein's written reports. See Saul Friedländer, *Kurt Gerstein: The Ambiguity of Good* (New York: Alfred A. Knopf, 1969), originally published in Europe in

1967 by Casterman; and Pierre Joffroy, *A Spy for God: The Ordeal of Kurt Gerstein* (New York: Harcourt Brace Jovanovich, 1971).

3. *Enron CFO Andrew Fastow boasted*: See Russ Banham, "How Enron Financed Its Amazing Transformation from Pipelines to Piping Hot," *CFO*, October 1, 1999. To review the Securities and Exchange Commission complaint against Fastow, which describes his financial engineering, see United States District Court, Southern District of Texas, Houston Division, United States Securities and Exchange Commission, Plaintiff, v. Andrew S. Fastow, Defendant, Civil Action No. 17762, October 2002. As of this writing, the document was online at http://www.sec.gov/litigation/complaints/comp17762.htm. Fastow pleaded guilty in January 2004 and was sentenced to six years in prison.

4. *The disputed University of Colorado win*: The Missouri-Colorado game is described in many places. For example, see Jim Brady, "Colorado's Fifth-Down Score Stands; Missouri's Consolation: Officials Suspended," *Washington Post*, October 9, 1990.

5. *At Nuremberg, Nazi officials defended their actions as legal*: The quote about "dutiful little boys" comes from Colonel Howard Brundage, deputy chief of the U.S. War Crimes Office and the interrogator of foreign minister Joachim von Ribbentrop. See Robert E. Conot, *Justice at Nuremberg* (New York: Harper & Row, 1983), 90. The quote by Sir Hartley Shawcross appears in *Justice at Nuremberg* (p. 181), as well as online in the full text of Sir Hartley's presentation, dated December 4, 1945: http://history1900s.about.com/gi/dynamic/offsite.htm?site=http%3A%2F%2Fwww.courttv.com%2Fcasefiles%2Fnuremberg%2Fshawcross.html.

6. *Attached to actions . . . attached to consequences*: In ethical philosophy, Kant's approach is referred to as "deontological" and Bentham's as "teleological." For the sake of simplicity, we rely on lay terms—i.e., action-based and consequence-based ethics.

7. *Kant's categorical imperative*: See Immanuel Kant, "Fundamental Principles of the Metaphysics of Morals (1785)," in *The Right Thing to Do*, ed. James Rachels; The Heritage Series in Philosophy, ed. Tom Regan (New York: Random House, 1989), 95.

8. *Bentham's philosophy of utilitarianism*: See John Stuart Mill, "Utilitarianism (1861)," in *The Right Thing to Do*, 81.

9. *Doctors' beliefs about compliance*: Many (and in some cases most) physicians readily justify deception of third-party payers if it serves the interests of patients. See Victor G. Freeman et al., "Lying for Patients: Physician Deception of Third-Party Payers," *Archives of Internal Medicine* 159, no. 19 (1999): 2263–2270.

10. *The five most dangerous words*: Buffett gave this advice in a memo to his top managers. See Karen Richardson, "Buffett Says to Avoid Scandals, Managers Must Not Follow Herd," *Wall Street Journal*, October 10, 2006.

11. *Survey of taxpayers*: See IRS Oversight Board, *2005 Taxpayer Attitude Survey* (Washington, DC: IRS Oversight Board, 2005), question 4; available online at http://www.ustreas.gov/irsob/reports/2006/02212006.pdf.

12. *Experiments conducted by Solomon Asch*: See Solomon E. Asch, "Effects of Group Pressure upon the Modification and Distortion of Judgment," in *Groups, Leadership and Men*, ed. H. Guetzkow (Pittsburgh, PA: Carnegie Press, 1951), 177–190.

13. *"No controlling legal authority"*: Al Gore may have escaped legal trouble, but he could not explain away his ethical transgression. See Charles Krauthammer, "Gore's Meltdown," *Washington Post*, March 7, 1997. A transcript of Gore defending his actions is available online at http://cnn.tv/ALLPOLITICS/1997/03/03/gore.reaction/transcript.html.

14. *Philip Zimbardo's prison experiment*: For the information in this chapter, we relied on Philip G. Zimbardo et al., "A Pirandellian Prison: The Mind Is a Formidable Jailer," *New York Times Magazine*, April 8, 1973. We also cite information from a more academic article: Craig Haney, Curtis Banks, and Philip Zimbardo, "A Study of Prisoners and Guards in a Simulated Prison," *Naval Research Reviews* (1973). For an online summary of the experiment, see http://www.prisonexp.org/.

15. *A physician interviewed about the T4 program*: See Robert Jay Lifton, *The Nazi Doctors: Medical Killing and the Psychology of Genocide* (New York: Basic Books, 1986), 57.

16. *Nothing in the world is more dangerous*: See Martin Luther King Jr., *Strength to Love* (New York: HarperCollins, 1963), 46.

17. *"A gardener cultivates his plot"*: See James Allen, *As a Man Thinketh* (New York: Wildside Press, 2005), 11–12; originally published by Grosset & Dunlap, 1918.

Chapter 3

1. *Lao Tzu quote*: See Lao Tzu, *Tao Te Ching* [The book of the way].

2. *Ali Hasan's struggle with favoritism*: Hasan was a student in Ron Howard's ethics class in 2006. Although his name has been changed to protect his privacy, excerpts of his code, at both the beginning and the end of the chapter, are reprinted with his permission.

3. *The ten yamas, or "restraints"*: The full list of ten *yamas* includes *ahimsa* (noninjury), *satya* (truthfulness), *asteya* (nonstealing), *brahmacharya* (celibacy or fidelity), *kshama* (patience), *dhriti* (perseverance), *daya* (compassion), *arjava* (nondeception), *mitahara* (moderation), and *shaucha* (avoiding impurity). Although some of the *yamas* are expressed in positive form, they can also be expressed as "shall nots." For one overview of the *yamas*, see Sri Swami Sivananda, *All About Hinduism* (Uttarakhand. India: Divine Life Society, 2003). A useful online primer and resource is at http://veda.wikidot.com/.

4. *Buddhism's five precepts*: The five precepts often take the form of a five-part pledge: "I take upon myself the precept of abstention from killing . . . stealing . . . sexual misconduct . . . falsehood . . . all types of intoxicants causing negligence." The precepts may also be worded in a positive way—e.g., honesty instead of abstention from falsehood. A grounding principle of all five precepts is empathy. For a useful discussion, see Lily de Silva, "The Scope and Contemporary Significance of the Five Precepts," in *Buddhist Ethics and Modern Society*, eds. Charles Wei-hsun Fu and Sandra A. Wawrytko (New York: Greenwood Press, 1991), 143. See also Lawrence C. Becker and Charlotte B. Becker, eds., *Encyclopedia of Ethics*, vol. 1 (New York: Garland Publishing, 1992), 103.

5. *Muhammad's farewell sermon*: The University of Southern California maintains a useful compilation of Muslim texts. For the Prophet Muhammad's Last Sermon, see http://www.usc.edu/dept/MSA/fundamentals/prophet/lastsermon.html.

6. *A saint meditating in the forest*: Kausika, an ascetic, took the vow "I must always speak the truth." Following the story, the *Mahabharata* makes one of the main points of this chapter: "Many persons say, on the one hand, that the scriptures indicate morality. I do not contradict this. The scriptures, however, do not provide for every case." See "Karna Parva," book 8, section 69–71. The *Mahabharata* is available online at http://www.sacred-texts.com/hin/maha/index.htm.

7. *The Qur'an urges selflessness*: For this passage in the Qur'an, see University of Southern California, USC-MSA Compendium of Muslim Texts, Translations of the Qur'an, chapter 2: Al-Baqara (The Cow), verse 083, online at http://www.usc.edu/dept/MSA/quran/002.qmt.html#002.083.

8. *Story of the tortoise and merchants*: The tortoise fable is depicted in stone in a cemetery in Borobudur, Indonesia. It is one of the Jatakas, or stories of previous lifetimes of the Buddha. As of this writing, images and stories were available online at http://www.borobudur.tv/avadana_04.htm.

9. *Mother Teresa's mission*: This mission, widely attributed to Mother Teresa, was articulated by Archbishop Sean Brady of Ireland in 2003. For the comment, see "Blessed Teresa's Thanksgiving Day Is 'Perfect Ending' to Knock Pilgrimage Season," *Western People* (Ballina, Ireland), October 29, 2003. For the full flavor of Mother Teresa's philosophy, refer to her Nobel Lecture given on December 11, 1979. See Tore Frängsmyr, editor-in-charge, and Irwin Abrams, ed., *Nobel Lectures, Peace 1971–1980* (Singapore: World Scientific Publishing, 1997). Online, see http://nobelprize.org/nobel_prizes/peace/laureates/1979/teresa-lecture.html.

10. *Dalai Lama's Nobel lecture*: The lecture was given on December 11, 1989. For the full text, see http://nobelprize.org/nobel_prizes/peace/laureates/1989/lama-lecture.html.

11. *Weaknesses of the Golden Rule*: Authors Sissela Bok and Rushworth Kidder point out some of the Golden Rule's limitations. See Bok's essay on the Golden Rule in Ted Honderich, ed., *The Oxford Companion to Philosophy* (Oxford: Oxford University Press, 2005), 321. See Kidder's comments in Rushworth M. Kidder, *How Good People Make Tough Choices: Resolving the Dilemmas of Ethical Living* (New York: Quill, 2003), 160.

12. *Inconsistencies in the Golden Rule*: One example is in Islam. In Muhammad's Farewell Sermon, he says, "Hurt no one so that no one may hurt you." But in the Hadiths, quoted earlier, he says, "No one of you is a believer until he desires for his brother that which he desires for himself." Religious texts used in Christianity and Judaism are similarly inconsistent. "Love thy neighbor as thyself" appears in Leviticus 19:18, but in the book of Tobit 4:15, we find "Do that to no man which thou hatest."

13. *Counselor Polonius gives advice*: See William Shakespeare, *The Tragedy of Hamlet, Prince of Denmark*, scene 3. The text of *Hamlet* is online at http://www-tech.mit.edu/Shakespeare/hamlet/full.html.

14. *Gandhi pleaded for restraint*: See K. L. Tuteja, "Jallianwala Bagh: A Critical Juncture in the Indian National Movement," *Social Scientist* 25, nos. 1–2 (January–February 1997): 25–61.

15. *When McCartney claimed victory*: Bill McCartney later expressed remorse at his decision, as reported by CNN/*Sports Illustrated* in 1998. See "McCartney 'Remorseful' About Fifth-Down Play," *Sports Illustrated*, June 20, 1998. Online, see http://sportsillustrated.cnn.com/football/college/news/1998/06/20/mccartney_fifthdown/.

16. *Game between Dartmouth and Cornell*: The story of the Cornell forfeit has been told many times. A play-by-play retrospective with comments by Cornell's quarterback shows how Cornell's act of sportsmanship has reverberated for decades as a benchmark of ethical behavior. See Bob Duffy, "Men of Honor: When 1940 Cornell Football Team Gave Back Fifth-Down Victory, Players Went from Winners . . . To Losers . . . To Bigger Winners," *Boston Globe*, December 29, 2001. The wording of Cornell's telegram comes from a

story online at IvyLeagueSports.com, http://www.ivyleaguesports.com/documents/cor-041106 .asp.

17. *West Point honor code*: The West Point code offers an explicit discussion of the nuances of lying, cheating, and stealing. See United States Army, United States Corps of Cadets, "The Honor Code and System" (Department of the Army, 2004). The code is online at http://www.usma.edu/Cpme/documents/USCC%20PAM%20632-1.pdf.

18. *Nelson Mandela exacted no retribution*: The quote by Mandela comes from an interview with Oprah Winfrey, apparently on a show aired on December 25, 2000. The quote appears in a news report on *The Oprah Winfrey Show* on Independent Online, a South African Web site. See http://www.iol.co.za/index.php?set_id=1&click_id=3&art_id=ct20010 321211006717K316249/. *BBC News* also reports this quote, not attributing when it was made. See "Profile: Mandela's Magic Touch," *BBC News*, August 28, 2001. Online see http://news.bbc.co.uk/2/hi/africa/1513244.stm.

19. *Benjamin Franklin's thirteen virtues*: See Benjamin Franklin, *The Autobiography of Benjamin Franklin*, eds. Leonard W. Labaree, Ralph L. Ketcham, and Helen C. Boatfield (New Haven, CT: Yale University Press, 2003), 149–150. The autobiography is also online at http://www.bartleby.com/1/1/4.html.

20. *See United Nations Web site*, http://www.un.org/Overview/rights.html.

21. *Three rules of thumb*: See United States Corps of Cadets, "The Honor Code and System," 1–4.

22. *Painful decision in Taiwan*: The story of facilitating payments comes from an interview by Bill Birchard with James Baker, retired CEO of Arvin Industries, in 2002. See Bill Birchard, "Global Profits and Ethical Perils," *Chief Executive*, June 2002, 29–34.

23. *Ethics code for coaches*: The U.S. Olympic Committee's Coaching Ethics Code is available online at http://www.usoc.org/education/ethics.pdf.

24. *American Medical Association code*: The American Medical Association's Principles of Medical Ethics, as amended June 17, 2001, is online at http://www.ama-assn.org/ama/pub/category/2512.html.

25. *American Bar Association's model rules*: See rule 1.6 in the American Bar Association's Model Rules for Professional Conduct from the Center for Professional Responsibility, online at http://www.abanet.org/cpr/mrpc/mrpc_toc.html.

26. *Story of the whaleship Essex*: See Nathaniel Philbrick, *In the Heart of the Sea: The Tragedy of the Whaleship Essex* (New York: Penguin Books, 2000), 174.

27. *President James K. Polk's deception*: See Richard Shenkman, "Presidential Improprieties," *Baltimore Sun*, January 24, 1999. The story of Polk's deception is also in Michael Farquhar, *A Treasury of Deception* (New York: Penguin Books, 2005), 110.

28. *"Show me the spot"*: See Stephen R. Jendrysik, "History Reveals War Is Always Unpopular," *Republican*, December 14, 2005.

29. *The Church of England condoned slavery*: Author Adam Hochschild tells the story of the elimination of the slave trade in England. In the eighteenth and nineteenth centuries, the trade was a foundation of the country's economy, and leaders of all stripes overlooked its evil. See Adam Hochschild, *Bury the Chains: Prophets and Rebels in the Fight to Free an Empire's Slaves* (Boston: Houghton Mifflin, 2005), 61–68.

30. *George Washington remained a slave owner*: The story of George Washington and Sir Guy Carleton also comes from Hochschild, *Bury the Chains*, 101, 102.

31. *Charles Barkley, role model*: Barkley was fined and suspended for the spitting incident. In spite of his behavior, he was revered as a player, and in 2006 he was inducted into the Basketball Hall of Fame. See "NBA Fines and Sits Barkley for Spitting," *Newsday*, March 29, 1991; and David Aldridge, "Barkley Caps Career with Hall of Fame Call," *Philadelphia Inquirer*, April 3, 2006.

32. *Paul Hamm won a contested gold medal*: The entire controversy, reported widely in the press, is explained in detail in the ruling by the Court of Arbitration for Sport, or CAS. See Michael J. Beloff, Dirk-Reiner Martens, and Sharad Rao, "Arbitration Between Mr Yang Tae Young and Korean Olympic Committee v. Paul Hamm, U.S. Olympic Committee, et al.," ed. Court of Arbitration for Sport (2004).

33. *Aleksandr Solzhenitsyn*: See Aleksandr I. Solzhenitsyn, *The Gulag Archipelago: 1918–1956* (New York: HarperPerennial, 2002), 312.

34. *Famous Islamic hadith*: See it online at http://www.al-islam.org/fortyhadith/1.htm.

Chapter 4

1. *Aristotle quote*: Aristotle, *Nicomachean Ethics* (350 BCE), book 2, chapter 1.

2. *Over 850 million people*: The actual number in 2006 was 854 million, according to the Food and Agriculture Organization. This included 9 million people in industrialized countries. See Food and Agriculture Organization, *The State of Food Insecurity in the World 2006* (Rome: Food and Agriculture Organization of the United Nations, 2006), 8.

3. *Thousands die in armed conflicts*: According to "global burden of disease" estimates by the World Health Organization (WHO) data, 171,000 people died in 2002 from armed conflicts. This data is derived from annual reports by the WHO. As of this writing, the most recent data was at http://www.who.int/research/en/. A dated report from the United Nations puts the cumulative number of child deaths in armed conflict over a decade at 2 million. See *Impact of Armed Conflict on Children*, available online at http://www.un.org/rights/introduc.htm#contents. Deaths from armed conflict make up about 0.5 percent of all deaths annually. See C. J. L. Murray et al., "Armed Conflict as a Public Health Problem," *British Medical Journal* 324 (2002): 324.

4. *"I only wrote this long"*: This quote is attributed to many authors. Blaise Pascal may deserve the most credit. He wrote (in French), "Je n'ai fait celle-ci plus longue que parce que je n'ai pas eu le loisir de la faire plus courte." See Blaise Pascal, *Texte Primitif de Blaise Pascal* (Paris: Adamant Media Corporation, 2006), 300.

Chapter 5

1. *Benjamin Franklin*: See Benjamin Franklin, *The Writings of Benjamin Franklin*, Vol. 5, Albert Henry, ed. (New York: Macmillan 1907), 437.

2. *Six men were infused with TGN1412*: The story of the reaction of the clinical-trial subjects to TGN1412, along with the subsequent emergency treatment, is chronicled by the supervising physician at Northwick Park Hospital. See Ganesh Suntharalingam et al., "Cytokine Storm in a Phase 1 Trial of the Anti-CD28 Monoclonal Antibody TGN1412," *New England Journal of Medicine* 355, no. 10 (2006): 1019–1020.

3. *Observers asked why put healthy men at risk*: For an early critique, see Michael Goodyear, "Learning from the TGN1412 Trial," *British Medical Journal* 332 (2006): 677–678. The questions raised by the study had been raised beforehand by ethics experts concerned about novel kinds of research. See Carol Levine et al., "'Special Scrutiny': A Targeted Form of Research Protocol Review," *Annals of Internal Medicine* 140, no. 3 (2004). Two of the same authors reiterated their concerns after the debacle. See Carol Levine and Jeremy Sugarman, "After the TGN1412 Tragedy: Addressing the Right Questions at the Right Time for Early Phase Testing," *Bioethics Forum* (online journal) This article is online at http://www.bioethicsforum.org/20060417clevinejsugarman.asp.

4. *Authorities cleared researchers of wrongdoing*: The TGN1412 case did not result from drug researchers run amok. The question was whether the researchers identified and made skillful decisions about all the ethical issues before they proceeded. See the follow-up report by British drug regulators: Medicines and Healthcare Products Regulatory Agency, *Investigations into Adverse Incidents During Clinical Trials of TGN1412* (London: Medicines and Healthcare Products Regulatory Agency, 2006), 2. In a letter of defense, TeGenero's chief scientific officer reported on the company's careful (but apparently inadequate) work before launching the clinical trial. See Thomas Hanke, "Correspondence: Lessons from TGN1412," *Lancet* 368 (2006), 1569–1570.

5. *TGN1412 was a novel drug*: TeGenero had documented the risk of a cytokine storm in its drug application to government authorities: TeGenero, *Investigator's Brochure: TGN1412 Humanized Agonistic Anti-CD28 Monoclonal Antibody* (Würzberg, Germany: TeGenero AG, 2005), 10, 52. Documents related to the TGN1412 case are available online at http://www.circare.org/foia5/tgn1412.htm.

6. *The test bristled with ethical questions*: For an in-depth discussion of problems with the consent form, see Norman M. Goldfarb, "Informed Consent in the TeGenero TGN1412 Trial," *Journal of Clinical Research Best Practices* 2, no. 5 (2006).

7. *A simple decision-making process*: These steps are adapted from the principles of decision analysis, a field pioneered by author and Stanford professor Ron Howard. For more detail, see Ronald A. Howard "Decision Analysis: Practice and Promise," *Management Science* 34, no. 6 (June 1988): 679. Also see Ronald A. Howard and James E. Matheson, *The Principles and Applications of Decision Analysis* (Menlo Park, CA: Strategic Decisions Press, 1984). Professor Howard's next book on decision analysis is at press. See Ronald A. Howard and Ali E. Abbas, *Foundations of Decision Analysis* (Upper Saddle River, NJ: Prentice-Hall, 2008).

8. *Was the researchers' decision bad?*: The question of whether TGN1412 researchers should have waited was raised many times. For example, see Goodyear, "Learning from the TGN1412 Trial"; Levine and Sugarman, "After the TGN1412 Tragedy"; and Alastair J. J. Wood and Janet Darbyshire, "Injury to Research Volunteers—The Clinical-Research Nightmare," *New England Journal of Medicine* 354, no. 18 (2006): 1869–1871.

9. *Her teenage son's forays on the Internet*: This example is adapted from a case cited by Rushworth Kidder at a talk he gave in Palo Alto, California, in March 2007. In the case, the woman decided to read her child's e-mails. Kidder is president of the Institute for Global Ethics, Camden, Maine. See http://www.globalethics.org and Rushworth M. Kidder, *How Good People Make Tough Choices: Resolving the Dilemmas of Ethical Living* (New York: Quill, 2003).

10. *A nurse visiting an elderly patient*: Among nurses caring for cancer patients, lying and deception are common. Research shows that nurses often see no alternative if they are to prevent harm and provide compassion. The quoted case is reprinted, with permission, from A. Tuckett, "Bending the Truth: Professionals' Narratives About Lying and Deception in Nursing Practice," *International Journal of Nursing Studies* 35 (1998): 296. Copyright © Elsevier 1998.

11. *Gerstein tried many ways to overcome*: Gerstein's discipline and courage were undeniable. He didn't compromise easily. See Saul Friedländer, *Kurt Gerstein: The Ambiguity of Good* (New York: Alfred A. Knopf, 1969), 51–52, originally published in Europe in 1967 by Casterman.

12. *Of the party he wrote*: Ibid., 59.

13. *Kant's three formulations*: Kant went on to elaborate the second formulation: "It is clear that he who transgresses the rights of men intends to use the person of others merely as a means, without considering that as rational beings they ought always to be esteemed also as ends, that is, as beings who must be capable of continuing in themselves the end of the very same action." See Immanuel Kant, "Fundamental Principles of the Metaphysics of Morals (1785)," in *The Right Thing to Do*, ed. James Rachels; The Heritage Series in Philosophy, ed. Tom Regan (New York: Random House, 1989), 99. Kant argued explicitly against consequentialism: "Thus the moral worth of an action does not lie in the effect expected from it, nor in any principle of action which requires to borrow its motive from this expected effect"; see Kant, "Fundamental Principles," 94. Also see Immanuel Kant, *Groundwork of the Metaphysics of Morals*, trans. Mary J. Gregor, with contrib. Christine M. Korsgaard (Cambridge, MA: Cambridge University Press, 1998), 14.

14. *The TGN1412 consent form*: A thorough discussion of the consent form appears in Goldfarb, "Informed Consent."

15. *Decision made by executives at Google*: The Google case is summarized in a Business Roundtable publication: Kirsten E. Martin, *Google, Inc., in China* (Washington, DC: Business Roundtable Institute for Corporate Ethics, 2006). Online, see http://www.darden.edu/corporate-ethics/pdf/BRI-1004.pdf. Another excellent source is Clive Thompson, "Google's China Problem (and China's Google Problem)," *New York Times Magazine*, April 23, 2006, 64–71, 86, 154–156. We build on the publicly available facts to draw lessons from the Google experience.

16. *Decision-making analysis*: For an in-depth discussion of decision-making analysis beyond the scope of this book, see Howard and Abbas, *Foundations of Decision Analysis*.

17. *Google's action outraged many*: Politicians in the United States had a field day in using Google as a whipping post. Google shared politicians' ire with Yahoo! and Microsoft, which also do business in China. See the transcript of all oral congressional testimony quoted in this chapter, including the comments of both Tom Lantos and Elliot Schrage: Subcommittee on Africa, Global Human Rights and International Operations and the Subcommittee on Asia and the Pacific Committee on International Relations, U.S. House of Representatives, "The Internet in China: A Tool for Freedom or Suppression?" 109th Congress, Second Session, February 15, 2006, online at http://commdocs.house.gov/committees/intlrel/hfa26075.000/hfa26075_0f.htm.

18. *Schrage's written testimony*: The testimony, published by Google, is online at http://googleblog.blogspot.com/2006/02/testimony-internet-in-china.html.

Chapter 6

1. *German businessman John Rabe*: For the story of John Rabe and the attack on Nanking, we rely entirely on Iris Chang, *The Rape of Nanking* (New York: Penguin, 1998), 111, 116, 117, 119, 160, 173, 189, 191. Some people put the number of civilians killed at 350,000 (see Chang, p. 4). The story of Rabe, a Nazi outside Germany, shows how skillful ethical thinking stems from our reasoning abilities and not national origin.

2. *Six-year-old George Washington*: See Mason Locke Weems, *The Life of Washington*, ed. Marcus Cunliffe (Cambridge, MA: Belknap Press, 2001), 12. The text of the book is also online at http://xroads.virginia.edu/~cap/gw/weems.html.

3. *A human being annihilates his dignity*: See Immanuel Kant, *The Metaphysics of Morals*, ed. Mary J. Gregor, Cambridge Texts in the History of Philosophy (1996; repr. Cambridge: Cambridge University Press, 2000), 182.

4. *Studies show that people in romantic relationships*: See Rim Cole, "Lying to the One You Love: The Use of Deception in Romantic Relationships," *Journal of Social and Personal Relationships* 18, no. 1 (2001): 125.

5. *Is it true; is it kind; is it useful?*: The origin of this advice is unclear. It appears in the writings of C. W. Leadbeater. However, it closely follows a passage in the Tipitaka, a part of Theravada Buddhist scripture: "Monks, a statement endowed with five factors is well-spoken, not ill-spoken. It is blameless and unfaulted by knowledgeable people. Which five? It is spoken at the right time. It is spoken in truth. It is spoken affectionately. It is spoken beneficially. It is spoken with a mind of good-will." Sutta Pitaka, Anguttara Nikaya 5.198. The Tipitaka is online at http://www.accesstoinsight.org/tipitaka/index.html.

6. *A story told by a nurse*: See A. Tuckett, "Bending the Truth: Professionals' Narratives About Lying and Deception in Nursing Practice," *International Journal of Nursing Studies* 35 (1998): 298. Copyright © Elsevier 1998.

7. *Deception of dying people*: See Sissela Bok, *Lying: Moral Choice in Public and Private Life* (1978; repr. New York: Vintage Books, 1999), 231.

8. *Skillful handling of promises*: See Robert C. Solomon and Fernando Flores, *Building Trust: In Business, Politics, Relationships, and Life* (New York: Oxford University Press, 2001).

9. *Before acting, we inform our partner*: See Sue Shellenbarger, "'Honey, I'm Thinking of Having an Affair': Therapists Advise Confessing Temptation," *Wall Street Journal*, October 16, 2006.

10. *Loyalty's strong hold on us*: See Bok, *Lying*, 149.

11. *Russian gymnast Irina Karavaeva*: Irina Karavaeva's story received little attention in U.S. media and didn't make much of a splash in the sports world. In the arbitral ruling by the Court of Arbitration for Sport for Paul Hamm, the judges cited her precedent but so misspelled her name (as "Ka Aaeva") that her story remained buried. For a news report on her relinquishing the gold to Dogonadze, see Susan Carver, "Gymnastics: 'Noble' Russian Gives Gold Medal to Beaten Rival," *Independent (London)*, August 22, 2001. Her record is published on the International Gymnastics Federation Web site at http://www.fig-gymnastics.com/events/athletes/bio.jsp?ID=3542. Her award for fair play is recorded on the International Fair Play Committee Web site at http://www.fairplayinternational.org/winners_item.php?id=606. As of this writing, Karavaeva had won twenty-five World Cup victories.

12. *Woman arrested for not paying taxes*: The authors' recollection of a story published many years ago, probably in the *San Jose Mercury News*.

13. *Parable of the Sadhu*: This story is adapted and reprinted by permission of *Harvard Business Review*. From "The Parable of the Sadhu," by Bowen H. McCoy, May–June, 1997. Copyright © 1997 by the Harvard Business School Publishing Corporation: all rights reserved. This article was originally published in 1983: Bowen H. McCoy, "The Parable of the Sadhu," *Harvard Business Review*, September/October 1983.

14. *Closing chapter in the Rabe story*: See Chang, *The Rape of Nanking*, 194–195.

Chapter 7

1. *Quote by Shakespeare*: William Shakespeare (1564–1616), *Measure for Measure*, act 3, scene 1 (1603 or 1604).

2. *Story of Outcome Software*: The passages about Outcome Software are from the personal experience of author Clint Korver. Korver founded Outcome in 1997. He passed the CEO job to another manager in 2000. Korver departed in 2003, and Outcome closed in 2004. The only employee who left during the early periods with cash flow shortages was a single mother who needed a more secure source of income.

3. *Survey data from LRN*: On the Web, see LRN, "New Research Indicates Ethical Corporate Cultures Impact the Ability to Attract, Retain and Ensure Productivity Among U.S. Workers," August 3, 2006, http://www.lrn.com/content/view/263/175/.

4. *Thirty-six percent of people say they have left a job*: Ibid.

5. *Annual surveys of trust in professions*: See Wendy Koch, "Poll: Washington Scandals Eating Away Public Trust," *USA Today*, December 11, 2006.

6. *United Way of the National Capital Area*: The United Way story is based on reporting by Bill Birchard in April 2005 and May 2007, including two interviews with CEO Charles Anderson. Birchard's work initially appeared in *CFO* magazine: Bill Birchard, "Nonprofits by the Numbers," *CFO*, July 2005, 50–55. For those interested in an exhaustive exposé of lying, deception, and graft at a charity, the forensic audit makes fascinating reading. See PricewaterhouseCoopers, "United Way of the National Capital Area Forensic Accounting Investigation" (Washington, DC: PricewaterhouseCoopers LLP, August 7, 2003).

7. *Critics' ammunition to attack*: The *Washington Post* ran an article and an editorial on Anderson's management. See Jacqueline L. Salmon, "United Way Official Resigns, Alleges Inflated Numbers," *Washington Post*, May 22, 2006; and Editorial, "A Stumble at United Way," *Washington Post*, May 29, 2006.

8. *Always tell the truth*: This is similar to a Mark Twain quote and apparently erroneously attributed to him. The actual Twain quote: "Always do right. This will gratify some people and astonish the rest." Mark Twain [Samuel Langhorne Clemens] (1835–1910), February 16, 1901, to Young People's Society, Brooklyn. *The Columbia World of Quotations* (New York: Columbia University Press, 1996).

9. *Story from the food industry*: This story, included anonymously to protect the individual's privacy, happened in 2000.

10. *Concept of a "quality" commitment*: This concept was developed by author Ron Howard, on the basis of work by Fernando Flores, the former minister of finance for Chile.

Flores developed a concept called action language. For a profile of Flores's approach, see Harriett Rubin, "The Power of Words," *Fast Company*, December 1998, 142.

11. *Taxi driver Osman Chowdhury*: The story of Osman Chowdhury from the BBC was one of the most complete. See Salim Rizvi, "Bangladesh Cabbie Is Toast of NYC," *BBC News*, February 9, 2007, http://news.bbc.co.uk/2/low/south_asia/6345901.stm. As of this writing, a video of Chowdhury was posted at http://video.msn.com/v/us/msnbc.htm?f=00&g =6eabc8d8-a1db-4b04-8185-c807ceaf1fed&p=hotvideo_m_edpicks&t=m5&rf=http://www .msnbc.msn.com/id/17024253/&fg=.

12. *The example of Matthew Farmer*: The story of Matthew Farmer was recounted in Nathan Koppel, "Lawyer's Charge Opens Window on Bill Padding," *Wall Street Journal*, August 30, 2006. Farmer tallied the bill padding in a letter to a judge in Minneapolis. See Matthew I. Farmer, Letter to Judge Janet Poston, Re: Connecticut Specialty Ins. Co. v. Pinnacle Corp., et al., CT-03-015259, February 20, 2006.

13. *A bill-padding survey in 2007*: See Nathan Koppel, "Study Suggests Significant Billing Abuse," *Wall Street Journal Online*, May 1, 2007, http://blogs.wsj.com/law/2007/05/ 01/study-suggests-significant-billing-abuse/. See the *Wall Street Journal* blog for many follow-up comments: http://blogs.wsj.com/law/2007/05/01/study-suggests-significant-billing-abuse/.

Epilogue

1. *Friedrich Nietzsche's predicament*: This notion, known in philosophy as *eternal recurrence*, appears in several places in Nietzsche's writings. The quote comes from Friedrich Nietzsche, *Nietzsche: The Gay Science: With a Prelude in German Rhymes and an Appendix of Songs*, ed. Bernard Williams (Cambridge: Cambridge University Press, 2001), 194.

2. *Top-rated violinists have practiced*: See K. Anders Ericsson and Neil Charness, "Expert Performance: Its Structure and Acquisition," *American Psychologist* 9, no. 8 (1994): 741.

3. *Johannes Brahms interview*: See Arthur M. Abell, *Talks with Great Composers* (New York: Carol Publishing Group, 1994), 5, 6.

4. *A human being is a part*: This quote by Einstein comes from a letter dated 1950, as quoted in Howard W. Eves, *Mathematical Circles Adieu and Return to Mathematical Circles* (Washington, DC: Mathematical Association of America, 2003), 60.

Ron Howard, a professor at Stanford University, began teaching ethics nearly three decades ago. His ethics courses have been filled to capacity for many years. He has made a name for himself by helping students recognize ethical distinctions they had never before considered. Never one to abide flimsy logic, he is a keen adviser about ethical decisions in work and life.

Howard is a professor in the Department of Management Science and Engineering. A member of the National Academy of Engineering, he has been since 1980 the director of the department's Decisions and Ethics Center, which examines the efficacy and ethics of social arrangements. Howard is also a founder and chair of the board of the Decision Education Foundation, whose goal is to improve the lives of young people by teaching them how to make better decisions.

Since the 1960s, as a professor at both Stanford and MIT, Howard has defined the profession of decision analysis. He has in the meantime applied his principles to projects ranging from investment planning and research strategy to hurricane seeding and nuclear-waste isolation. His experience has given him the perspective and know-how for tackling the most difficult ethical issues of the day.

Howard was also a founding director and longtime chairman of Strategic Decisions Group (SDG), a firm specializing in decision-making processes in the pharmaceutical, electric utilities, automotive, and other industries. The author of three books and dozens of technical papers, he is professor by courtesy in Stanford's Graduate School of Business.

Clint Korver is a serial entrepreneur in Silicon Valley and an expert in decision making. He is the CEO and founder of DecisionStreet, an Internet company building Web-based tools to help consumers make important life decisions about health, wealth, housing, and family affairs. He is also a founder and partner at Decision Quality International, a training and consulting firm that helps leaders in organizations make and cause better decisions. Although Korver has successfully built four companies based on Howard's unique decision-analysis ideas, some of his most memorable achievements have come from the skillful handling of ethics in business.

Korver entered the field of decision analysis and ethics in 1989 as a doctoral student of Professor Howard. He earned his PhD from the Engineering Economic Systems Department at Stanford University in 1994 and immediately began starting and building companies. He has also taught ethical decision making as a visiting professor at Grinnell College, where he now serves as vice chair of the college's board of trustees. He works with Howard at the Decisions and Ethics Center at Stanford University in the Department of Management Science and Engineering, and he sits on the advisory board of the Decision Education Foundation, which teaches decision-making skills to K–12 students.

Korver's professional and academic leadership roles put him in constant touch with people facing thorny ethical issues. Like Howard, Korver has a reputation for adeptly drawing a bright line between ethical and unethical behavior—and using ethical decision making to transform work and life for the better.

For more help in developing a personal ethical code and making ethical decisions, go to www.ethicsfortherealworld.com.